WYNNSTAY & THE WYNNS.

A VOLUME OF VARIETIES.

PUT TOGETHER BY THE AUTHOR OF

"THE GOSSIPING GUIDE TO WALES."

OSWESTRY:

PUBLISHED BY WOODALL AND VENABLES,

BAILEY HEAD AND OSWALD ROAD.

1876.

In the interest of creating a more extensive selection of rare historical book reprints, we have chosen to reproduce this title even though it may possibly have occasional imperfections such as missing and blurred pages, missing text, poor pictures, markings, dark backgrounds and other reproduction issues beyond our control. Because this work is culturally important, we have made it available as a part of our commitment to protecting, preserving and promoting the world's literature. Thank you for your understanding.

SIR WATKIN WILLIAMS WYNN, BART., M.P.

CONTENTS.

ILLUSTRATIONS.

TO

LADY WILLIAMS WYNN

THIS BOOK

IS RESPECTFULLY DEDICATED BY

THE PUBLISHERS.

MARCH, 1876.

OUR ILLUSTRATIONS.

THE collotype of Wynnstay is taken from a photograph by Mr. Maclardy, of Oswestry; and the one of Llangedwyn from a photograph by Mr. Owen, of Newtown. The wood-engravings are re-produced from Dean Howson's *Valley of the Dee*, published by Virtue and Co., and originally issued in the *Art Journal*. The collotype of the old mansion of Wynnstay, as it appeared after the fire, is copied from a picture in Lady Williams Wynn's scrap book. The lithographs of Sir Watkin and Lady Williams Wynn, and the autotypes of the Misses Williams Wynn, are from French photographs, kindly lent to the publishers by Sir Watkin. The portraits of the first and second baronets are from family pictures at Wynnstay by Allan Ramsay and Sir Joshua Reynolds. We are indebted to the courtesy of Mr. Wynne of Peniarth for our likeness of the third Sir Watkin, the latest painting of him having been destroyed by the fire at Wynnstay in 1858.

PEDIGREE OF SIR WATKIN WILLIAMS WYNN, BART.

S IR Watkin Williams Wynn, of Wynnstay, in the county of Den-
bigh, was born May 22nd, 1820; and succeeded to the
Baronetcy, he being the sixth baronet, upon the death of his father,
January 6th, 1840.

I.—THE FAMILY OF THE WILLIAMSES.

Cadrod Hardd was a chieftain whose seat was in the Isle of Anglesey. He is
styled Lord of Talebolion, and had several sons, one of whom, Idhon ab Cadrod,
was the founder of this family.

Idhon, the fourth son of Cadrod Hardd, a British Chieftain who was also,
lord of Talebolion. The eleventh in descent from Idhon ab Cadrod was

Evan ap William, a gentleman, of Bryngwallon, in the county of Anglesea, father,
by Margaret his wife, daughter of Edward ab Jevan, to William Williams, Gent, of
Brynygwallon, (¹), who married Catherine, daughter of Richard ab Hugh ab William,
and had several children, one of whom was Evan Williams, Gent., Chwaenisaf,
Anglesey, who died about 1562, father by Janet his wife, daughter of John Gwilym,
B.D., to

William Williams, Gent., Chwaenisaf, who married Margaret, daughter and heiress
of John Owens, Llanfaethlu, Anglesey, and had issue,

I. John Williams, Gent., Chwaenisaf, founder of the Williamses, of Chwaenisaf,
who are extinct.

II. Hugh, the second son, viz.—

The Rev. Hugh Williams, B.D., of Nantanog (²), Anglesey, vicar of Llantrisant,
who was born in 1596, and died in 1670, leaving by Emma his wife, who was daughter
and heiress of John Dolben, Caegwynion, Denbighshire, and niece to the Bishop of
Bangor, of the family of Segroit, a son,

William Williams, an eminent lawyer, Recorder of Chester, and Speaker of the
House of Commons, in the reign of Charles II. He was knighted by James II., on
his appointment to be Solicitor-General, and made a Baronet July 6th, 1688. Sir
William was put on his trial, when Speaker of the House of Commons, on a charge
which was brought against him in the Court of King's Bench, viz., ordering to be
printed, as Speaker of the House, the report of Thomas Dangerfield, Gent. He was
fined £10,000, although he pleaded the privileges of Parliament, and that he was
acting in obedience to the House. Sir William was chosen one of the Privy Council
after the Revolution, and ended his patriotic career by bringing in the Treating Act,

---

(1) William ab Evan, ab William, ab Iolyn, ab Adam ab Einion, who was called Adda ab Einion Velyn in the reign of
Edward III. (1362).
(2) The Rev. H. Williams, D.D., who held the Rectory of Llanrhyddlad, April 15th, 1633, and was Prebend of Faenol
in the Cathedral Church of St. Asaph, and a Canon in the Cathedral Church of Bangor. He died Sept. 21st, 1670,
aged 74 years.

which afterwards became law and continues still to be one of the bulwarks that surround the purity of the British Parliament. He married Margaret, daughter and heiress of Watkin Kyffin, Esq., Glascoed, Llansilin, who descended from Einion Efell, lord of Cynlleth, illegitimate son of Madock, Prince of Powis. By this lady, who transferred the Glascoed estate to the family of her husband, Sir William left two sons and one daughter,

    I. William, his heir.

    II. John, of Chester, and Bodelwyddan, barrister-at-law, who married Catherine, eldest daughter of Sir Hugh Owen, Bart., of Orielton, and had issue,

        1st. Hugh, M.P. for the county of Anglesea, who married, first, Ursula, daughter of Sir John Bridgeman, Bart.; second, a daughter of Edward Norris, M.D., and M.P. for Liverpool; and died without issue.

        2nd. Kyffin, who married Mary Bunbury, and died without issue.

        3rd. John, a Welsh Judge, and great great grandfather to Sir Hugh Williams, the present Baronet of Bodelwydden (3).

        4th. Arthur, Archdeacon of St. David's, who died without marrying.

        5th. Edward, who in 1739 married Jane, daughter and heiress of Lewis Owen, Esq., of Peniarth, Custos Rotulorum for Merionethshire, and relict of Richard, 5th Viscount Bulkeley. They had three daughters; Jane, the eldest, married William Wynne, Esq., of Wern.

        6th. Elizabeth, married to Sir William Owen, of Orielton, Bart., M.P. for Pembrokeshire.

    III. Emma, married to Sir Arthur Owen, Bart.

Sir William died July 11th, 1700, and was succeeded by his eldest son, Sir William second baronet. This gentleman married, first, Jane, daughter and heiress of Edward Thelwall, Esq., of Plasyward, Ruthin, by Sidney, his second wife, daughter and heiress to William Wynn, son of Sir John Wynn, of Gwydir, (4), who was made a baronet June 29th, 1611. Through this connection Sir William Williams left three sons, besides two daughters, viz.—

    I. Watkin, his heir.

    II. Robert, of Erbistock (5), in the county of Denbigh, M.P. for Montgomeryshire, who married Meryel, daughter of Arthur Williames, of Ystymcolwyn, Esq., but died without issue in 1763.

    III. Richard of Penbedw (6) Denbighshire, who left by Charlotte, his second wife, daughter and heiress of Richard Mostyn, Penbedw (third son of Sir Roger Mostyn), one son who died young; also by Annabella, his third wife, daughter and heiress of Charles Lloyd, Esq., Trenewydd, Shropshire, four sons, who all died without issue, (the eldest, Watkin, who was Lord Lieutenant of Merionethshire and Denbighshire, died in 1808), and two daughters, of whom—

        1st. Annabella, married to the Rev. Philip Puleston, D.D., of Pickhill, Denbighshire. She had two daughters, co-heiresses:

            Annabella, married first to Edward Lloyd Lloyd, Esq., (formerly Kenyon), who, in obedience to the will of Watkin Williams, Esq., uncle of his wife by the

(3) Here the family of Wynnstay and that of Bodelwyddan branched off, and they continued so until they were re-united by the marriage of Sir Hugh Williams with the present Sir Watkin's sister.

(4) Gwydir, or more properly Gwaed-dir, from a battle which was fought there by Llywarch the Aged, about the year 510. The old house stood at the foot of Carreg-y-gwalch, where lived an outlaw, named David ab Jenkin, in the time of the Wars of the Roses. His hiding-place is still known as David ab Jenkin's cave.

(5) Erbistock is situated on the borders of Flintshire and Denbighshire, and of English Maelor. This parish belonged formerly to the Abbey of Bangor Iscoed.

(6) Penbedw is situated in the manor of Penbedw, in the parish of Nannerch. This manor was given in 1544, by Henry VIII. to Peter [Pyers] Mostyn, of Talacre, on paying in hand £73. There was formerly at this hall a large library, which, with others, came into the possession of W. W. E. Wynne, Esq., of Peniarth, who is considered no mean authority in antiquarian lore.

mother's side, adopted the surname and coat of arms of Williams. She married for her second husband, General Thomas Molyneux, K.H., who also adopted the surname and coat of arms of Williams.

Elizabeth married William Wynne, Esq., of Peniarth, Merionethshire. She was mother to the present possessor, William Watkin Edward Wynne, Esq.

2nd. Jane, married to Robert Lloyd, Esq., of Swan Hill, Oswestry, and had one son, Robert Watkin, who died s.p., and two daughters—Annabella, who married with Edward Gatacre, of Gatacre, Esq.; and Jane, who married with John Wynne Eyton, of Leeswood, Esq.

Sir William married for his second wife Catherine, daughter of Mutton Davies, Esq., of Gwysaney, Flintshire, and had no issue. He died October, 1740, and was succeeded by his eldest son,

Sir Watkin, third baronet, M.P. for Denbighshire, who succeeded to Wynnstay under the will of Sir John Wynn, Bart., in consequence of which he adopted the additional surname and coat of arms of Wynn. He married, first, Ann, daughter and heiress of Edward Vaughan, Esq., of Llwydiarth and Llangedwyn, M.P. for Montgomeryshire, who was heir of O. Vaughan, Esq., Llwydiarth (7), and Catherine his wife, daughter and heiress of Maurice Roberts, Esq., of Llangedwyn. Sir Watkin, married for his second wife Frances, daughter of George Shakerley, Esq., of Gwersyllt, Denbighshire, by whom, who died in 1803, he had two sons. Sir Watkin's death was caused by a fall from his horse whilst hunting near Acton Park, Wrexham, September 20th, 1749. He was succeeded by his eldest son,

Sir Watkin, fourth baronet, M.P. for Denbighshire. This gentleman married, August 6th, 1769, Lady Henrietta Somerset, fifth daughter of Charles, fourth Duke of Beaufort. She died a few months afterwards. He married for his second wife, December 21st, 1771, Charlotte, daughter of the Right Hon. Geo. Grenville, Prime Minister of England, and sister to the Marquis of Buckingham and Lord Grenville. She died in 1832, and had issue,

I. Watkin, his heir.

II. The Right Hon. Charles Watkin, of Llangedwyn, member of the Privy Council, M.P. for Montgomeryshire, D.C.L., and F.S.A., born Oct. 9th, 1775, and married April 9th, 1803, Mary, eldest daughter of Sir Foster Cunliffe, Bart. She died June 14th, 1838, and had issue,

1st. Watkin Henry, born June 29th, 1816, died July 9th, 1832.

2nd. Charles Watkin, the present M.P. for Montgomeryshire, born October 24th, 1822, married the Lady Annora Pierrepont, daughter of Charles, Earl Manvers, and has issue.

3rd. Charlotte.

4th. Mary, married to James Milnes Gaskell, Esq., of Thornes, Yorkshire.

5th, Harriet Hester, married to John Lindsay, Esq., Loughry, Tyrone, Ireland.

6th. Sidney, married to Sir Francis H. C. Doyle, Bart, and died in November, 1867.

III. The Right Hon. Sir Henry Watkin, G.C.H., ambassador to the Court of Denmark, married in 1813 to the Hon. Heather Smith, sixth daughter of Lord Carrington.

Sir Watkin died in July, 1789, and was succeeded by his eldest son,

Sir Watkin, fifth baronet, M.P. for Denbighshire, Lord Lieutenant of the counties of Denbigh and Merioneth, was born Oct. 26th, 1772, and married Feb. 4th, 1817, the

---

(7) Llwydiarth is situated in the parish of Llanfihangel y Gwynt or Gwynva. It formerly belonged to the great family of Vaughan, descended from Aleth the Aged, King of Dyfed.

Lady Henrietta Antonia Clive, eldest daughter of Edward, Earl of Powis, and sister to Charlotte Florentia, Duchess of Northumberland. Lady Henrietta died December 22nd, 1835, and had issue,

I. Watkin, the present baronet, married April 28th, 1852, to his cousin, Marie Emily, daughter of Sir Henry W. Williams Wynn, of Llanvorda.

II. Herbert Watkin, born April 29th, 1822, and married Anna, only daughter and heiress of Edward Lloyd, of Cefn, Esq., and died 22nd June, 1862, leaving issue—

    1st. Edward Watkin, born 1857.
    2nd. Herbert Lloyd Watkin.
    3rd. William Robert Herbert Watkin.
    4th. Florentia Helen.

III. Henrietta Charlotte, married April 16th, 1843, to Sir Hugh Williams, the present baronet of Bodelwyddan.

The late baronet died January 6th, 1840.

This family quarter their coat of arms, the Wynns, (that of Owen Gwynedd), and the Williamses. Seats: Wynnstay, Glanllyn, near Bala, Llangedwyn, Llwydiarth, Llanforda, near Oswestry.

2.—THE FAMILY OF THE WYNNS.

To the house of Gwydir, one branch of which on the female side is represented by Williams Wynn of Wynnstay, must be accorded the highest rank in the genealogies of Wales. This ancient family can trace their pedigree in a straight male line through Roderick, lord of Anglesey, son of Owen Gwynedd, Prince of North Wales, to Anarawd, King of North Wales, eldest son of Roderick the Great, King of Wales. The latter succeeded to the principality of Powis and the kingdoms of Gwynedd and South Wales. He was killed in 876, and left, by Angharad his wife (sister and heiress of Gwrgan ab Merick, lord of Cardigan), three sons—

I. Anarawd ab Roderick the Great.
II. Cadell ab Roderick the Great, King of South Wales.
III. Mervin ab Roderick the Great, Prince of Powis, who died 900.

The eldest son, Anarawd, King of Gwynedd, whose seat was at Aberffraw, Anglesea, died in 913, leaving issue—1st, Idwal Voel ab Anarawd; 2nd, Ellis ab Anarawd. Anarawd was succeeded by his eldest son,

Idwal Voel, King of Gwynedd, who was killed, together with his brother Ellis, in 940, whilst fighting against the Danes. By his cousin Avandreg, daughter to Mervin, Prince of Powis, Idwal left issue; with others, his eldest son,

Merick ab Idwal Voel, who was taken prisoner in 977. He had his eyes taken out, and was shut up in prison, where he died, leaving a son,

Idwal ab Merick, who in 992 was raised by the people to the throne of Gwynedd, from which he had been driven by Meredith ab Owen, Prince of Powis. In the following year Sweyn, a Danish chieftain, landed in Gwynedd, and Idwal was killed in the act of opposing him. His only son,

Jago ab Idwal, was dethroned by Llywelyn ab Seisyllt, husband of Angharad, Queen of Powis, but was restored in 1021, after the death of that prince. Jago was killed in 1037, in a battle fought between him and Griffith, son of Llewelyn ab Seisyllt. He left a son,

Cynan ab Jago; he was expelled from his throne by Griffith ab Llywelyn, who also took possession of the kingdom of South Wales. Cynan died, after making two unsuccessful efforts to regain his throne, leaving his eldest son,

Griffith ab Cynan, who after many attempts to recover the government of his country, formed a treaty in 1079 with Rees ab Tewdwr, Prince of South Wales. The contending Princes met on the mountains of Carno ([8]), and there a battle was fought, which ended in the defeat and death of the usurper, Trahacrn, and the restoration of Griffith and Rees. Griffith died in 1136, at the age of eighty-two, and was interred in Bangor Cathedral, after reigning 57 years. He married Angharad, daughter of Owen ab Edwin, lord of Tegeingl, and had issue—1st, Owen Gwynedd ; 2nd, Cadwaladr ab Griffith, lord of Cardigan, who died in 1172. Griffith was succeeded by his eldest son,

Owen Gwynedd, Prince of Gwynedd, a celebrated warrior, who after a successful reign of 32 years, died in December, 1169, and was interred at Bangor. Owen married twice—first, with Gwladys, daughter of Llywarch ab Trahaern, lord of Pembroke, and through her was father to

Iorwerth (Edward) Drwyndwn, who was expelled from the throne, first, by his illegitimate brother Howell; and afterwards by his brother David, son of Owen Gwynedd by his second wife. Edward died at Pennant Melangell ([9]), Montgomery-shire. He married Margaret, daughter of Madock, Prince of Powis, and had one son,

Llywelyn ab Iorwerth, surnamed the Great, who in 1194 claimed and obtained with-out a struggle his paternal crown from his uncle David ab Owen Gwynedd. David married the lady Emma Plantagenet, sister to King Henry II. of England -

"" David, King Owen's son, my father's son,
He wed the Saxon, the Plantagenet !"—*Southey*.

Llywelyn died in 1240, after a remarkable reign of 36 years, and was interred in the Abbey of Conway. His grandson, Llewelyn ab Griffith, the last Prince cf Wales, was killed by the English near Builth, December 11th, 1282.

Owen Gwynedd married for his second wife his cousin Christian, daughter of Grono ab Owen ab Edwin, lord of Tegeingl, and had issue, second son,

Roderick ab Owen, lord of Anglesea, a prince of great authority, who married Agnes daughter of Rees ab Tewdwr Mawr, King of South Wales, and had children ; with others,

Thomas ab Roderick, lord of Ffriwlyd, who married the widow of Owen Brogyntyn lord of Edyrnion, and daughter of Einion ab Seisyllt, lord of Merioneth. Thomas was father to

Caradock ab Thomas, lord of Ffriwlyd, who, by Eve his wife, daughter of Gwyn ab Griffith ab Beli, had issue,

Griffith ab Caradoc, lord of Friwlyd, who married Leuci, daughter of Lywarch Vaughan, ab Lywarch Goch, ab Lywarch Holburch, and was father to

David ab Griffith, whose wife was Eve, daughter and heiress of Griffith Vaughan, of Penyved, in Evioneth. From the issue of this marriage, the third son,

Howell ab David, married Eve, daughter and heiress of Evan ab Howell, of Cefnyfan, descended from Collwyn ab Tango, lord of Evioneth ; and had a son,

Meredith ab Howell, who lived in the reign of Edward III. He married Morvydd, daughter of Evan ab David, of Lleyn, of the royal tribe of South Wales, and was succeeded by his eldest son,

Robert ab Meredith, who, when he was eighty years of age, married Angharad daughter of David ab Llywelyn, of Cefn-Melgoed, South Wales, and was father to

---

(8) Carno, Montgomeryshire. A battle was fought in this neighbourhood, in 948, between Evan and Jago, the sons of Idwal Foel, and the sons of Howell the Good, which ended in the defeat of the latter ; also in 1077, between Griffith ab Cynan, who was assisted by Rees ab Tudor, Prince of South Wales, and Trahaern ab Caradock, aided by Caradock ab Griffith and Meilir, sons of Riwallon ab Gwyn, his relatives, Trahaern and his followers fell, and victory declared for Griffith, who took possession of his lawful throne. There is a tradition still extant in the neighbourhood about these battles, and it is said the " Carnedd " on the Garn mountain was erected in commemoration of these remarkable events.
(9) Iorwerth Drwyndwn was killed near a place called Bwlcheroes Iorwerth.

Evan ab Robert, who married Catherine, daughter of Rees ab Howell Vaughan, and had a son,

Meredith ab Evan, who bought Gwydir of David ab Howell Coetmore ([10]). Meredith died in 1525. By his first wife Alice, daughter of William ab Griffith ab Robin, of Cochwillan ([11]), he had, with other children, a son,

John Wynn, ap Meredith, of Gwydir, Carnarvonshire, who died in 1553. He married Ellen Lloyd, daughter of Maurice ab John ab Meredith, of Penmorva, and he had by her, with other children,

Maurice Wynn, of Gwydir, who married twice. ˚By his second wife, Catherine, daughter and heiress of Tudor ab Robert Vaughan, of Berain—descended from March-weithian, lord of Isaled.–-he was father to Edward Wynn, of Ystrad, founder of the Wynns of Llwyn (who were represented in the female line by the late Rev. Lloyd Wynne, of Nerquis, Flintshire). By his first wife Jane, daughter of Sir Richard Bulkeley, Knight, of Beaumaris, Maurice Wynn was father to

Sir John Wynn, Bart., of Gwydir, who was born in 1553, and made a baronet in 1611; he was author of the "History of the Gwydir Family." Sir John married Sydney, daughter of Sir William Gerard, Chancellor of Ireland, and died March 1st, 1626-7, after having issue,

I. Sir Richard Wynn, Bart., Gwydir, who married Ann, daughter and heiress of Sir Francis Darcy, of Isleworth. Sir Richard died without issue in 1649, aged 61 years, and was succeeded by his brother,

II. Sir Owen Wynn, Bart., Gwydir, who married Grace, daughter of Hugh Williams, of Wīg, and left a son and successor,

Sir Richard Wynn, Bart., Gwydir, who married Sarah, daughter of Sir Thomas Myddelton, Bart., of Chirk Castle, and had an only daughter,

. Mary Wynn, who married with Robert, Marquis of Lindsay, Lord Willoughby d'Eresby, and afterwards Duke of Ancaster.

After the death ot Sir Richard, who had no male issue, he was succeeded by his cousin,

Sir John Wynn, Bart., who married Jane, daughter and heiress of Eyton Evans, of Wattstay (Wynnstay) and died without issue, January 7th, 1719, when the baronetcy ceased.

III. William Wynn, Esq., Prothonotary of Wales (sixth son of Sir John Wynn, the first Bart.), married the daughter and heiress of Thomas Lloyd, of Gwernybrechtyn. By her he was father to

Sidney Wynn, who married with Edward Thelwall, Esq., of Plasyward, Ruthin. Their daughter,

Jane Thelwall. This lady was married to Sir William Williams, Bart., Llanforda, and was mother to Sir Watkin, the third Bart., who, after Sir John Wynn, the last baronet of the Gwydir line, possessed the Wynnstay estate and adopted the surname and coat of arms of Wynn. From them Sir Watkin Williams Wynn the present baronet (as previously shown) is descended. The paternal grandmother of Jane Thelwall was the Lady Margaret Sheffield, a daughter of Edmund, Earl of Mulgrave, K.G.

([10]) Coytmore, or the Big Wood, is situated in the parish of Llanllechyd, Carnarvonshire. The estate now belongs to Lord Penrhyn.

([11]) William ab Griffith ab Robin, of Cochwilan, which place is in the same parish, and is demolished, with the exception of its fine old baronial hall, which is still standing. He raised a troop of horse, and followed Henry VII to the Battle of Bosworth. He was made, for his valuable services, Sheriff of Carnarvonshire for his life, and continued so until 1496.

AVENUE IN WYNNSTAY PARK.

WYNNSTAY AND THE WYNNS.

A LITTLE more than a century and a half ago, when Sir John Wynn, of Watstay—rapidly approaching the ninetieth year of his age, and totally blind—was wheeled in his chair every morning from his mansion to the great oak in the park that he might touch it ; at that period, we say, it was by no means certain who would succeed the aged baronet as owner of the noble park ; a park then, as we are told, so thickly grown with timber as to be thought unhealthy as a residence. Sir John, unlike most men, who put off making their " last will and testament" until they are almost past performing the act, had quite a penchant for making wills, several of which he executed during his long career. Sometimes one kinsman would be the favourite, then another, and at one period of his life it was a Cholmondeley that seemed likely to be selected as the fortunate successor. Thus, had Sir John died some years sooner than he did, the grandson of the famous Speaker, and great-grandfather of the present Sir Watkin Williams Wynn, would have died Sir Watkin Williams, and the park and mansion, then newly called Wynnstay, would have passed into other hands.

It has been said that the place was once known as
Rhiwabon, but, if so, we cannot tell when the name was
changed to Watstay, or, indeed, why it was so changed,
although the presumptive evidence is because the mansion
stands on Wat's Dyke, which runs through the park.
Gough, however, in his dreadfully personal and therefore amusing *Memoirs of Myddle*, says :—" Stanwardine
is sold to Sir John Win, of Watstay, so called from
Wat or Walter stopping here." Once called ' Watstay'
the transition to ' Wynnstay' is obvious enough, but even
here there are all sorts of traditions afloat amongst our
elders, which would be received with due respect were
there any obscurity in the matter, and the name Wynnstay a thousand years old.

Still these old stories are worth noting. One, auda-
ciously setting known facts at defiance, has it, that a
gentleman of the name of Wynn, offering his hand and
heart to the heiress of the estate, was duly accepted.
One night when he would have left the mansion to go
home, after paying a visit to his ladye-love, the storm raged
outside with such fury that he was urged to remain, but
all to no avail, until the heiress, clasping her hands
before him, with a look that went to his heart, exclaimed,
" Oh, Wynn, stay !" A better tradition than this is one
that has long been current, and which gives the Devil a
hand in the naming of the mansion. The story goes that
for some purpose or other the Evil One wanted a ditch
from sea to sea, to accomplish which he engaged a
couple of the numerous army of willing workers he always
has at command ; but with the peremptory orders that
their job was to be completed between sunset and sunrise.
Whether the diggers were unused to the work, or were
lazy, or the task was too great for the time specified, we

are not told ; whatever the reason may have been, long before they had gained the shore, one of them, lifting himself up to " straighten his back," saw the approach of day, on which he placed his hand on his comrade's shoulder, and said, " Ween-stay ;" and thus it was "the Devil's Dyke" was never completed, and the Wynns got a name for their mansion.

And before we fairly commence our sketch of the Wynn and Williams families, as we are on the subject of old stories (for they can scarcely be dignified by the name of traditions), let us give another relative to one of Sir Watkin's estates. " Y Bwch yn ucha," one of the mottoes of the Wynnstay family, is said to have arisen thus :—There once lived at Llwydiarth two brothers, bachelors, who were owners of that estate and manor. Being out one day hunting, one of them saw a child under a holly bush, and a goat standing (rampant, as in the crest) over the little one. The old bachelor took the child home, adopted him, and gave him the name " Celynin Vychan, Bwch yn Ucha." Another version has it that this child was called Watkyn, and that he became a famous lawyer, who, by his wonderful genius managed to convert all the farmsteads of Llanfihangel (which only paid his patron chief-rents, as lord of the manor), into freeholds of the Llwydiarth estate ; and the legend points proudly to the proof of its veracity in the fact that the crest has a holly bush and a huntsman's staff on it bearing the goat company.

But it is time we came down to sedate and sober history. When we want to know everything about anything in Wales we naturally turn first to Pennant, and that usually accurate observer speaks of several houses that have, at different periods, stood on the site of the

present Wynnstay mansion ; the oldest recorded being
dated 1616.   In the time of the second Sir John Wynn,
of the Gwydir line, who became the first Wynn of
Wynnstay, there was, on a wall within a court, this
inscription :—

> *Wynn stay*, or rest satisfied with the good things providence
> has so liberally showered on you.

Of the several houses that have been known to exist on
the spot the most famous was, of course, the one that
was destroyed by fire in 1858, the particulars of which
sad calamity will be found in another part of this book.
In Pennant's time this was " the new mansion," and he
says it was only part of a more extensive design.   " It
is finished in that substantial yet neat manner becoming
the seat of an honest *English* country gentleman ; adapted
to the reception of his worthy neighbours, who may ex-
perience his hospitality without dread of spoiling the
frippery ornaments, becoming only the assembly-rooms
of a town house, or the *villa* of a great city."   Pennant
was a *bon vivant*, and, perhaps, had in his mind's eye,
when he wrote, wants and requirements such as do not
assimilate so well with the tastes of the more refined
age we live in.   At any rate, from his point of view, the
present mansion cannot be suitable for " an honest English gentleman"—at least for " one of the olden time,"
for its appointments are exceedingly choice and artistic.
Outside it has been described by an able artist as " a
rather severe adaptation of the Louis Quatorze style."
Much of the mansion of 1616 was standing in Pennant's
time, and part of it remained till the fire in 1858.

As true Welshmen of course we all rejoice that Sir
Watkin is *not* " an honest English gentleman," and the
pedigree we give shews that there has been little of the

WYNNSTAY.

Saxon in his line. " Sir John Wyn of Gwydyr," the first of the baronets of that name, was a celebrity in his day, and has left behind him valuable contributions to Welsh literature. His *History of the Gwydir Family* is curious and interesting. His character has been held up as all that was worthy, and decried as everything that was crafty. He was M.P. for the county of Carnarvon in 1596, one of the Council of the Marches of Wales, and created a baronet in 1611. Being "shrewd and successful in his dealings," people were led to believe he oppressed them, and, says Yorke, in his *Royal Tribes of Wales*, " it is the superstition of the place [Llanrwst] to this day, that the spirit of the old gentleman lies under the great waterfall Rhaiadr y Wennol, there to be punished, purged, spouted upon, and purified from the foul deeds done in his days of nature." Then it is recorded that in 1615, Sir John, having incurred the displeasure of the Council of the Marches, Lord Ellesmere, the Chancellor, was appealed to, but "the shrewd" baronet made his peace in the surest manner, by paying a bribe of £250. He was a man, evidently, who tried to make the best of both worlds, for after squaring the court with his bribe, and managing to keep his name on the Commission for Carnarvonshire, he made his peace with heaven by founding a hospital, endowing a school at Llanrwst, and giving up sundry tithes to support these charities. Sir John Wynn bore one of the great standards at the funeral of Henry, Prince of Wales. He died in 1626-7 at the age of seventy-three.

Whatever may have been Sir John's true character, there can be no doubt that he was a practical man of business, and it was only the year before he died that he had a scheme in prospect for reclaiming the Traeths situated at the junction of the counties of Carnarvon and Merioneth, a work accomplished many years later, as we all know, by Mr. Madocks. Sir John wrote to his kinsman, Sir Hugh Myddelton, on the subject, prefacing his letter with, " I may say to you what the Jews said to Christ, We have heard of thy greate workes done abroade, doe now somewhat in thine owne country ;" and then he propounds his scheme, offering to " adventure a brace of hundred pounds to joyne with Sir Hugh in ye worke." But with all his practical wisdom there was a tinge of superstition in the old baronet, for in one of his letters he gravely describes three stones near Conway, " one redd as blood, the other white, and the thyrd a little bluer then the white stone, standynge in triangle wiese," of which he says the " tradicion is that God Allmighty hath wrought in this place a miracle for increasynge of our fayth." And then he narrates the particulars hòw, for sabbathbreaking, three " faythless women " were turned to stone of the colour of the dresses they wore when they were " workynge uppon ye Saboathe day." Sir John considered that the tradition was wholesome " whether ytt was soe or noe," if only to " deterr others from workinge uppon the Saboath day."

Sir John's eldest son, Sir John Wynn, Knt., who died before him, accompanied Charles I., when Prince of Wales, upon that romantic expedition into Spain, when the Prince went to seek the hand of the Spanish Infanta. Sir John's second son, Richard, succeeded to the estates, and he was a "patron" of Inigo Jones, who, some writers believe, was a native of Wales. Richard dying without issue, the family honours devolved on his brother Owen, and when he was gathered to his fathers another Richard reigned in his stead. This Richard married the daughter of Sir Thomas Myddelton, of Chirk Castle, by whom he had a daughter only; and at his death the title went to his cousin, John, and this was the Sir John who, marrying the daughter of Eyton Evans, of Watstay, changed the name of the mansion and estate. Eyton Evans was the grandson of Thomas Evans, of Oswestry, attorney-general in the Court of the Marches. Sir John was "a man of pleasure in his youth," and late in life when he paid a visit to Court, in the early days of Queen Anne, we are told by Yorke of his meeting "after many years absence, his old Westminster school-fellow, the apostolic Beveridge of St. Asaph: 'Ah, Sir John, Sir John,' says the good bishop to him, 'when I knew you first the Devil was very great with you.' 'Yes, by gad, my lord,' says Sir John, 'and I wish he was half so great with me now.'" He died at the age of ninety-one, "and lies buried at Rhiwabon," says the same authority, "under a mass of marble, ludicrous to look on."

We must now say something about the Williamses, the direct ancestors of Sir Watkin. The head of the family was the not very bashful lawyer who became one of the most famous men of the age. Although the son of a clergyman of good family (his father being Dr. Williams, canon of Bangor), he did not possess much that would recommend him as a son-in-law to a country squire fond of money; nevertheless he won the lady of his choice from her calculating father. Being "on one of his Welsh circuits," Williams danced with the daughter of Walter Kyffin, of Glascoed, Oswestry, popped the question, and was referred to papa. "And what have you?" asked the stern parent, naturally anxious to know how the dancing lawyer meant to keep a wife. "I have sir, a *tongue* and a *gown*," replied the modest gentleman;

and the father was wise enough to see the force of the
reply.   Sir William Williams was an eminently successful man, who knew perfectly well how to look after the
main chance.   In the time of Charles the Second he was
Speaker, and in this capacity he signed an information
against one Dangerfield, which was treated as a libel,
and it cost him £8,000; but after the Revolution the
judgment was reversed by the House of Commons.
When Solicitor-General he conducted the prosecution of
the Seven Bishops, and failed to get a conviction, to the
no small joy of Jeffreys, who knew The Seal would go to
Mr. Solicitor if he should be successful.   The honour of
knighthood was conferred on him when he became
Solicitor-General in 1687, and in the following year he
was made a baronet.   Sir William died in 1700, at the
age of sixty-six, and was buried at Llansilin, near
Oswestry.
   It is said that the young barrister got into the good
graces of the parent Kyffin by winning a cause for him at
Salop assizes, and another story tells how being engaged
in the suit the validity of a deed came in question, on
which Mr. Kyffin said if the deed was his a sixpence
would be found within the seal; and so it was, and
the lawyer turned the circumstance to good account and
won a victory.   In 1675 Sir William Williams bought
Llanvorda, Oswestry, from the last of the Lloyds, who
said, writing to a friend, that he had no means to save
himself "but by being swallowed up by the great Levia-
than of our laws and lands."   The second Sir William
married into the Wynn of Gwydir family when he took
to wife Jane Thelwall, grand-daughter of William Wynn,
Prothonotary of Wales, sixth son of the first baronet of
Gwydir, and this lady became mother of the first Sir

SIR WATKIN WILLIAMS WYNN.

BORN 1692,   DIED. 1749.

Watkin Williams Wynn, of Wynnstay, who inherited the estates, and added the name of Wynn to that of Williams.

The last of the Gwydir family who resided at Wynnstay, was, as we have already said, blind in his later years. He died in 1719, and in 1720 the " Honour'd Watkin Williams," who took the additional surname of "Wynn," came into the estate. In some documents, the *Gentleman's Magazine,* for instance, he is sometimes called " The Honourable," but this is wrong. "The Honour'd" was equivalent to Esquire of high degree, in an age when the title of Esquire was not, as now-a-days, one "greatly affected by vulgar people." When Mr. Watkin Williams formally took possession of the estate there was much rejoicing, and at Wrexham an ox was roasted whole, one of the horns of which, set in silver, and bearing a suitable inscription, is at Wynnstay, and the other at Peniarth.

There are some curious records of The Honour'd Mr. Williams Wynn preserved in the old periodicals. In 1732, we are told "the livery servants of Watkin Williams Wynn, Esq., arm'd with Pistols on Horseback marched into Chester the 11th of October at the head of 900 Welshmen with Clubs Staves and other dangerous Weapons crying Down with the Rumps knocking down and wounding several persons." The master of these faithful retainers had arrived in the city before them, lending his aid to the Grosvenor party in an election, and the design of the Welshmen in following was said to have been to " protect the Magistrates in their Illegal Designs to make 300 Honorary Freemen." " The citizens, jealous of their rights, armed in their own defence and drove the Welshmen out of the city." But it would seem that this little breeze soon blew over, for in 1736 we find Mr. Wynn elected mayor of Chester, "at whose treat his lady presented 120 Services of Sweetmeats to that number of Citizen's Wives, valued 7s. 6d. each, and the feasting continued several days, insomuch that little business was done but by Cooks and Confectioners. Such appearence of gentlemen were never seen there since Lord Delamere was Mayor at ye Revolution." *(Gents. Mag.*, Oct. 1736).

In 1728 we find "Watkin Williams Wynn" mayor of Oswestry, and either then, or later on, he presented to the Corporation a silver punch ladle, which is still used in civic festivities. In 1732 he presented to Jesus College, Oxford, with which he had been connected, a silver-gilt bowl, containing ten gallons, which, at one time, we are told, was "filled with swig and handed round" on St. David's Day to those who sat at the festive board. Filled it might have been, but as to "handing round," that is quite another matter, for the bowl is so large in circumference that it is as much as a full-grown man can do to make his hands meet when he places his arms round it. It is still brought out on "Gaudy Days" we believe, but more for show than use, while another bowl, called the "Little Sir Watkin," is the one from which the votaries of St. David pay their devotions to their patron saint. This lesser vessel was not a gift of the Wynns, but of some ardent Welshmen who honoured the Principality in its design, for the bowl is supported by a bull-dog and a goat; the one represented as howling under his burden, whereas the latter bears it handsomely.

Sir William Williams, the son of the Speaker, dying in 1740, the "Honour'd" Mr. Wynn became the first Sir Watkin and third baronet, and in the general election of the following year he was nominated for Montgomery-shire and Denbighshire, but in the latter county the returning officer, William Myddelton, Esq., declared John Myddelton, Esq., duly elected. Sir Watkin petitioned, and the result was that he gained the seat, and the Returning Officer found himself in Newgate, where he lost not only liberty but an office he had held for two years (after the resignation of Edward Burton) viz. :—that of Receiver-General for North Wales. An old caricature representing Myddelton in Newgate was exhibited at the Cambrian Archæological meeting at Wrexham in 1875. The *Gentleman's Magazine* in April, 1742, gives the text of an address presented to Sir Watkin from the electors of Denbighshire and the Principality generally, thanking him for the efforts he had already made on behalf of the rights of voters and purity of elections, and pointing out sundry crying abuses that wanted correcting. Sir Watkin was every where hailed as a Patriot, and had he lived in our days would doubtless have been claimed as a Liberal. He was known as the " Great Sir Watkin," and it is said that when he went up to London to attend his Parliamentary duties, all the resident Welsh gentry came out as far as Finchley to meet him, where they formed into procession to escort the popular baronet into town.

Smollett describes the first Sir Watkin as " brave, open, hospitable," and the almost universal testimony concerning him is that he was amiable and just. There was one class, however, to whom his conduct was a trial ; but in estimating his behaviour to the Methodists we must bear in mind the age in which he lived, and we must remember, too, that the strange sect were con-scientiously believed to be lunatics by the upper classes generally. " The gentlemen," said Howel Harris, "hunt us like partridges." Whatever Sir Watkin did he did from want of knowledge rather than from want of heart. No doubt he fined the persons who attended the meetings of these new enthusiasts, right and left, for it is stated in the life of the Countess of Huntingdon that on her ladyship's laying the particulars before government, the fines were remitted, to the no small joy, and perhaps, triumph of the sufferers. Looking at the baronet's conduct and character 'all round,' we have no difficulty in believing that had he lived in our days, he would have been as generous in giving sites for meeting-houses as his warm-hearted and genial great-grandson is ; and remembering the age in which he lived, we ought to judge him by the light of it, and not of our day.

His death was caused by a fall from his horse whilst hunting near Acton, in the autumn of 1749, and thereby hangs a tale. It is said that his wife was very anxious he should not go out on that day, she having a presentiment that ill luck would happen ; some accounts say that her ladyship dreamt the orthodox number of three times that evil would befall her husband in that day's sport ; but he disregarded her warnings and was killed. Another story—and one that does not show that the Methodists were at all inclined to follow the Divine precept of turning the other cheek where one was smitten—tells us that just at the moment the baronet was killed sundry devotees were holding a Prayer Meeting, and one of the Brethren was offering up the following charitable petition to Heaven : " O Arglwydd cwympa Ddiawl mawr Wynnstay !" This becoming known, the story further informs us, that one large proprietor was so alarmed when he heard that he, too, was to be prayed for, that he at once

LLANGEDWIN HALL.

offered ground whereon to build a chapel, and so compounded with "the Jumpers!"

Sir Watkin was married twice; viz.: on the 20th November, 1715, at Llangedwyn, to Anne, daughter and co-heiress of Edward Vaughan, Esq., Llwydiarth and Llangedwyn, M.P. for Montgomeryshire; and secondly, in 1748, to Frances, daughter of George Shakerley, Esq. In reference to his second marriage it will be interesting to record, that in April, 1738, a fire broke out at Mr. Shakerley's mansion at Gwersyllt, near Wrexham, which was totally destroyed, the future lady of Sir Watkin being saved, with difficulty, after clinging for some time to a water-pipe outside her window. She survived her husband many years, and lived into the present century. And his first marriage reminds us of a story we have heard, that Llangedwyn Hall is said to have been built in the form of the letter "E," in compliment to Edward Vaughan, its owner.

Before we pass on to the next heir we 'must give an extract from a poem, dated 1751, that appeared in the *Cambrian Quarterly Magazine* in 1830, in which the praises of the first Sir Watkin were sung by a young Welshman, who was then only a clerk in the office of an "eminent country solicitor," at Nantwich, but who afterwards became Lord Chief Justice of England:—

There Watkyn stood, firm to Britannia's cause,
Guard of her ancient manners and her laws.
Oh, great good man! borne on the wings of fame,
Far distant ages shall revere thy name;
While Clwyd's stream shall lave the verdant meads,
And Snowdon's mountains raise their lofty heads;
While goats shall o'er thy hills, O Cambria! stray,
And day succeed to night, and night to day,
So long thy praise, O Williams, shall remain
Unsullied, free from dark oblivion's chain.

The future Lord Kenyon had not then discovered wherein his powers lay, and he soon ceased to pay court to the muses to attend courts where his services were better rewarded.

The second Sir Watkin, and fourth baronet, was only five months old when his father died. His mother, who survived him, made several valuable purchases on his behalf during his minority. Of these we may mention the Mathavarn estate, in 1752 (including the manor or lordship of Cyfeiliog), which, to quote an old chronicle, " belonged to the late Mr. Pugh," and was purchased " by the executors of the late Sir Watkin Williams Wynne, before a Master in Chancery, for £33,400," also the Rhiwsaeson estate. The manor of Cyfeiliog was granted in 1663 to John Pugh. It had previously been granted to Sir Thomas Myddelton. Touching these purchases we have the following particulars in the *Montgomeryshire Collections* of the Powys-land Club, for 1870 :—

"In 1737, John Pugh (Lord of the Manor of Cyfeiliog) died, leaving his niece, Maria Charlotte Pryce, wife of Thomas Pryce, his heiress-at-law, who, with her husband, in 1744, conveyed the manor with the ancient Mathavarn estate to James Lewis, Thomas Lloyd and John Morgan, upon trust to sell. And in 1754, by deed dated 2 and 3 May, the manor and estate were conveyed to Edward Kynaston, Esq., as a trustee for Sir Watkin Williams Wynn, Bart., then an infant. Four years afterwards (by Indentures dated 6 and 7 June 1758), William Owen, Esq., of Porkington, and Edward Kynaston, Esq., as trustees for Sir Watkin Williams Wynn, Bart., purchased the ancient Rhiewsaeson estate in Cyfeiliog from Margaret Owen.   .   .   . Thus passed this manor, comprising an area of upwards of 70,000 acres, and the extensive Mathavarn and Khiewsaeson estates into the possession of the House of Wynnstay."

Sir Watkin took to himself a wife when he was only twenty years of age, viz., the Lady Henrietta, daughter of Charles Noel Somerset, fourth Duke of Beaufort ; and

.he became a widower in three months. His portrait, by Reynolds, with that of the lady, painted the month before they were married, is preserved at Wynnstay. When he came of age, in the April of the following year, 1770, a Garagantuesque banquet was given in Wynnstay Park, at which it is said there were fifteen thousand guests. The amount of good things consumed on the occasion we give elsewhere, and we may add that, according to a MS. preserved at Wynnstay—a portion of which appeared in the *Annual Register* at the time—" three coaches full of cooks were sent from London for ye occasion." No expense seems to have been spared to make this coming-of-age a notable one, for what was afterwards known as the " Great Room," in the old Wynnstay mansion, was built for the festivities, and was only intended as a temporary erection, but so well-proportioned and convenient was it found to be, that it was allowed to remain, and bedrooms were built over it. Sir Watkin took to himself a second wife, December 21, 1771 ; Charlotte, daughter of the Right Hon. George Grenville, and sister of the Marquess of Buckingham ; a " beautiful and accomplished woman, twice painted by Sir Joshua." " How flexible are the affections of some men," says Mrs. Delany, in recording the event, " Sir W. W. W. the happiest of men : and *so he was* not *many months* with Lady Hart."

It was either during this year or the previous one that Garrick went to Wynnstay, " in obedience to many a pressing invitation," receiving in Shrewsbury, en route, some flattering proofs of his popularity. " For at Shrewsbury," we are told, " the whole town was in a ferment, and the Raven Inn, where the party put up, was besieged by the curious. When Garrick appeared, there was a crowd, who made free and rustic remarks on his person,

eye, hair, &c." A warm intimacy existed between the,
baronet and the actor, and Mr. Fitzgerald, in his *Life of
Garrick*, tells us of a present of cheese from Wynnstay,
accompanied by the following lines, in answer to some
that had been received from Garrick :—

> How fill'd were the Welshmen with envy and shame,
>   How each Bard for his character fear'd,
> When first they were told how immortal a name
>   In the list of all poets appear'd.
>
> *   *   *   *   *   *   *   *
>
> They send you these compliments greeting,
>   That if you'll permit them to hear you declaim,
> They'll stay from the next turnpike meeting, &c.

The biographer also says that he found amongst Garrick's
papers a " parody of the well-known Welsh song, and
beginning, ' Of a noble race was Sir Watkyn.'" We are
told in the same book that the picture of Garrick, by
Dance, (now at Sir Watkin's town mansion, in St. James's
Square,) was painted for Mrs. Garrick, the price being
fixed between the actor and artist at a hundred guineas,
but the baronet, unaware of this, offering a hundred and
fifty, became the fortunate purchaser.

The second Sir Watkin was very musical, and his name
may yet be seen, we believe, inscribed in Westminster
Abbey, as one of the promoters of the oratorios which
were performed in that building. He was fond, too, of
dramatic representations, and as early as 1770, the year
in which he came of age, Mr. Wright, in his *Caricature
History of the Georges*, records Sir Watkin's appearance
at Mrs. Cornely's masquerades, where he represented a
Druid. In 1773, we are told in Leslie's *Life of Reynolds*,
"the jolly Sir Watkin produced great effect (at a masquerade in the Pantheon), by riding in as St. David, mounted

SIR WATKIN WILLIAMS WYNN.

BORN. 1749,   DIED. 1789.

on a Welsh goat!" A few years later, when private theatricals became the rage, "the parties at Wynnstay were especially distinguished for their elegance." Several of the old play bills have been preserved, and copies of these—with some account of the performers—appeared in *Bye-Gones*, December 29, 1875. In Colman's *Random Records* interesting notices of the Wynnstay theatricals may be found; and no one knew more about the manner in which the performances were got up than did Colman the elder, for on several occasions he sustained the arduous post of stage manager. Not always, though, for a good story is told of Sir Watkin's perplexity when he took that office upon himself, in his difficulty in getting together the amateurs for rehearsal. "Who would be a stage manager!" said the baronet one day when all but deserted by his troupe. "Not I, Sir Watkin," replied a privileged retainer, "if I were owner of Wynnstay!" Admission to the Wynnstay Theatre was "by ticket only," and some of the tickets, from designs by Mr. Bunbury, are exceedingly clever. The earliest record we have of these performances is in 1780, but it was not until two years later that a regular theatre was built, and in a play bill for December, 1785, it is stated that "ladies are particularly requested to come without hats."

In one of the caricatures of the day, burlesqueing the distinguished amateurs whose hobby was Ancient Music, Sir Watkin is represented with a goat's face as a performer at a concert where the King and Queen are present amongst the audience. The other performers are well-known kindred spirits, and their " instruments," animals they are torturing to make them howl or otherwise utter discordant sounds. In 1775 we find him elected a member of the Dilletanti Society, which then had done

c

service, and was destined to do more, for the encouragement of Art.   In Sir Joshua Reynolds's picture of this
Club, painted in 1777, Sir Watkin is a prominent figure.

Sir Watkin was appointed Lord-Lieutenant of Merioneth in 1775, but the king does not seem to have taken
kindly to the choice of his minister.   " I consent to Sir
Watkin Williams (sic) being Lieutenant of Merioneth,"
his majesty writes, " if he means to be grateful ; otherwise, favours granted to persons in opposition is not very
political." (See Donne's *Letters of George III. to Lord
North*).   And here we may remark that up to the commencement of the present century the family was more
commonly styled " Williams," than " Wynn."   It is to
be presumed the baronet did shew the gratitude expected
during the fourteen years he held the appointment, for
his son, the third Sir Watkin, was installed in the office in
1793; and we find this son (who was also Lord-Lieutenant
of Denbigh) in 1810 at the head of five hundred Denbighshire Volunteers, doing honour to George III. by supporting Lord Kenyon on the occasion of his lordship's laying
the foundation-stone of Moel Vamma Tower, an extremely
ugly   monument   erected   in   commemoration   of   his
Majesty's jubilee.

Like his father, the second Sir Watkin was closely
identified with the town of Oswestry, and served the office
of mayor in 1774.   There is a race cup, too, given by
him and won by a horse belonging to Noel Hill, Esq.,
amongst the Oswestry corporation plate, which was presented to the borough somewhere about the time that the
latter gentleman was chief magistrate.

A Freemasons' Lodge was established at Wynnstay
by this Sir Watkin, some of the furniture belonging to
which is now used by the Lodge of St. Oswald, Oswestry.

But although so prominent as a musician, a patron of art, an amateur dramatic performer, and a mason, " the jolly" Sir Watkin is said to have been of a retiring disposition, possessing nothing of the energy of his father. He was an amiable man, much beloved, and he died in 1789, in the forty-first year of his age. His mother, as we have already said, survived him, and to his memory she erected the obelisk in Wynnstay Park, for which Sir Watkin's brother-in-law, Lord Grenville, wrote the inscription—*Filio optimo mater ehu superstes.*

We now come to the third Sir Watkin, the fifth baronet, and the father of the present owner of Wynnstay. He was born in 1772, and at the age of thirteen he appears as a " leading juvenile" at the Wynnstay Theatricals, and whilst yet a minor he came into the title, on the death of his father in 1789. He early in life exhibited great energy and activity, and a military ardour which no doubt the times developed and fostered. Soon after he came of age Sir Watkin raised a regiment of yeomen for active service, and it was gazetted in May, 1794 as the " Ancient British Fencibles." The regiment was first stationed at Gloucester, and on its march thither rested at Shrewsbury on the King's birthday, which was duly honoured by the men's drinking the health of his Majesty, at the expense of their commander. The original officers of this regiment included Mr. Richard Puleston (afterwards Sir Richard Puleston, Bart.) major; Mr. William Wynne, a relation of Sir Watkin, and father of the present Mr. Wynne, of Peniarth, Messrs. Richard Cummings, Gwyllim Lloyd Wardle and Edward Lloyd Lloyd, captains. No duty of any special importance was done by the Fencibles until 1798, when they assisted to quell the memorable Irish

Rebellion. In this outbreak "Sir Watkin's Lambs," or "The Bloody Britons," as they were severally called, did signal service, and it is said that for years afterwards the strains of the old Welsh air "Sir Watkin's Delight" always roused the angry passions of Irishmen. The most notable engagement in which they took part was the Battle of Newtown Barry, where, according to Musgrove, "Col. Williams Wynn advanced with the Ancient British Fencible Cavalry, which he commanded, to the front of the Infantry, and retook a gun which had fallen into the hands of the rebels." The regiment was also present at the Battle of Arklow, and made a dashing charge under their colonel, which redounded very greatly to their fame.

Sir Watkin's little band of volunteers suffered greatly in this rebellion. Young Apperley, who afterwards became a famous sporting writer under the nom-de-plume of "Nimrod," joined the regiment when it was in Ireland, and he says, "The severity of the losses of the Ancient British may be judged of by the simple fact of my having been gazetted youngest cornet on the 1st of April, 1798, and becoming nearly senior lieutenant in little more than a year and a half." Gwyllim Lloyd Wardle, who joined at the outset as captain, returned from Ireland lieutenant-colonel, and it is said that it was because the Duke of York would not incorporate the Fencibles with the regiments of the line that Colonel Wardle became a patriot! The men would have liked well enough to continue the trade of war for a longer period, for we find them early in 1799 presenting an address to Sir Watkin declaring their readiness to "follow him and his officers to the Continent, or any part of the globe, in the service of their king and country." This, however,

was not to be, and the regiment was disbanded at Wynnstay on the 2nd of May 1800,—marching from Wrexham
for that purpose. The Wrexham Yeomanry, and the
Rhuabon Light Infantry kept the ground, and the regiment being drawn up opposite the mansion Sir Watkin
thanked them for the loyalty, courage, and discipline
they had displayed during a period of six years' service,
and expressed to them his earnest wishes for their future
welfare. The standards were then deposited, and the
men dismounted, and the whole corps to the number of
four hundred dined in the " Great Room." After dinner
came the final parting, and this the men determined to
make a notable one, in spite of the entreaties of their
commander, by placing him in a chair and with loud
hurrahs, carrying him round the lines. This done, they
marched back to Wrexham, and the next morning
received their discharge.

When war's alarms had ceased, the leading spirits of
the regiment took to a variety of occupations, sporting
amongst the number. Thus, " A match between Lieut.-
Col. Wardle's ch. m. and Capt. Apperley's br. h. was run
over Chester Course, four miles, three hundred guineas,
which, after some very smart running, was won by the
former." And in the same month that saw the regiment
disbanded, we find it recorded that " the finest race ever
seen on Chester ground was for the gold cup, value £50.
The horses were Mr. Smith's bl. c. Sultan, 5 yrs. ; Sir W.
W. Wynn's Caper, 5 yrs. ; and Mr. Swenfin's b. c.
Tickler, 3 yrs." And, by the way, that race had a narrow chance of becoming memorable in other ways, for
Gamble, who rode Sir Watkin's horse, finding that
Tickler was winning the second heat easily, drew up at
the distance chain, with Phillips, who rode Sultan, and

the crowd, as usual, rushed within the ropes ; when sud-
denly, after walking half the distance, the two jockeys
tried for second place, and rode at speed amongst the
multitude, " by which means horses, jockeys, and several
people were thrown down, and three very dangerously
wounded." But Sir Watkin had other ways of occupy-
ing himself besides sporting. In 1806 he established an
" Agricultural Meeting" at Wynnstay, which for some
years was held every September, and was intended to
benefit the whole of North Wales. Prizes were awarded,
and the proceedings every year concluded with a dinner
for five or six hundred guests, so we need scarcely say
that the meeting was highly popular. In 1810, when
Lancasterian Schools were everywhere founded to meet
the requirements of an advancing age, Sir Watkin gave a
building in Wrexham " sufficiently large enough to edu-
cate five hundred poor children on the Lancasterian plan,
besides subscribing very handsomely towards the support
of the institution."

· The war fever, being strong again in England in
1814, revived in the breast of the Baronet all his old
military ardour, and we find him equipping for service
on the Continent, a regiment of Militia, and, at their
head, marching to France, prepared to fight his country's battles. He arrived just too late for the Battle of
Toulouse—the last great struggle before the capture of
the " Disturber of the Peace of Europe; " and, to the
great disappointment of officers and men, they all had to
return again without smelling powder. Very properly
the will was taken for the deed in England, and especially
in the Principality was the Cambrian hero honoured.
His reception by the Welsh in London on Saint David's
Day, 1815, was so enthusiastic that it is said the Prince

Regent, when Sir Watkin was presented to him, observed, " Surely you must be the Prince of Wales ! " " No, your Royal Highness," said Sir Richard Puleston, who was present, " Sir Watkin is the Prince *in* Wales ! " And in Wales he was everywhere received like a prince. When he made his appearance, by invitation, at Wrexham on the 18th of March, the horses were taken from his carriage, and their places supplied by the non-commissioned officers of his regiment, and such a crowd assembled in the streets that all idea of a " procession " had to be abandoned. At Bala, on the 11th of March, " although not expected, a vast crowd collected," as he stayed for a few minutes on his way to Glanllyn, and the horses were saved any further work. Congratulatory addresses, complimentary dinners, huge bonfires, distribution of food and clothing, rejoicings of all sorts, were the order of the day everywhere, culminating in the presentation, at Ruthin, of a silver vase, " weighing 1,500 oz., and costing 19s. 6d. per oz., measuring 3ft. 2in., by 2ft 4in. across, and containing 14 gallons," which was the gift of the county of Denbigh.

Sir Watkin and his fighting Welshmen did not return to take part in the final struggle of Waterloo, as some local historians state ; and Europe being at rest again, he turned his sword into a ploughshare and his spear into a pruning hook; but first of all he had a ceremony to go through of a highly interesting nature. In 1817 he was married to the Lady Henrietta Antonia Clive, and in 1820 the present baronet was born, when, as will be seen anon, the rejoicings customary in Wales and on the Border were celebrated on a scale of unusual extent. The pursuits of agriculture (to which Sir Watkin again returned) do not admit of much variety, but in 1820 Sir

Watkin tried an experiment in the growing of hops on his estate in Denbighshire, which, we presume, did not answer, or the practice would have been continued; and in the same year he won a gold medal from the Society for the Encouragement of Arts, &c., for planting, on the mountainous land near Llangollen, 80,000 oaks, 63,000 Spanish chestnuts, 102,000 spruce, 110,000 Scotch firs, 90,000 larch, 30,000 Wych elms, 30,000 mountain elms, 80,000 ash, and 40,000 sycamores.

During the autumn of 1832 Wynnstay was honoured with a Royal visit, and Sir Watkin entertained his future queen. In 1840 he died, this event being hastened by an accident he met with some months earlier in driving with Miss Frances Wynn, his sister, from Wynnstay to Nant-y-belan. They were thrown out of a pony carriage, and Sir Watkin was picked up insensible. Erysipelas set in, and he never thoroughly recovered. He was buried in Rhuabon Church, and the number of persons that attended his funeral was estimated by the newspapers of the time at ten thousand. An eye-witness informs us that the last carriage had not left Wynnstay when the first had arrived at Rhuabon; and hat-bands and scarfs were given to six hundred persons.

Having now performed the pleasant task of putting together the leading incidents in the career of the three former Sir Watkins, we prefer to avail ourselves more largely of the journalist's art in describing the career of the present popular and genial baronet, and condensing from the newspapers of the day the notable events in his life. But before we do so, there are a few last words we have to say of the family generally, and of Wynnstay in particular.

SIR WATKIN WILLIAMS WYNN.

BORN. 1772, DIED 1840.

Each Sir Watkin has in succession represented Denbighshire in Parliament. As Watkin Williams Wynn, Esq., the first of the baronets of the name of Watkin gained the seat in 1716 on the death of Sir Richard Myddelton, and he was re-elected, in 1722, after a hot contest with Robert Myddelton, Esq., who afterwards unsuccessfully petitioned against his return. He was again elected in 1727 and in 1732 ; and in 1741 came the final struggle we have already alluded to,—the " Election Mawr" that set at rest the rival claims of the houses of Wynnstay and Chirk Castle. The premature death of Sir Watkin, in 1749, left the seat vacant when the heir was only a few months old, and Sir Lynch Cotton was returned, and remained member—being twice re-elected—until 1774, when the second Sir Watkin took his place. Again, at his death, in 1789, there was no Sir Watkin old enough for the post, and Robert Watkin Wynne, Esq., of Plasnewydd, near Denbigh, now Plas Heaton, repre- sented the county until 1796, when Sir Watkin the third was returned. At his death in 1840 the same thing oc- curred again—the present baronet being under age—and the Hon. H. Cholmondeley kept the seat warm for him until the general election of 1841, when the fourth Sir Watkin entered Parliament. Where he has remained ever since, and he is not likely to be disturbed unless by removal to the upper chamber where electors cease from troubling and their lordships are at rest.

And here, let us remark, had Sir Watkin wished it he might have entered the House of Lords years ago. Addressing his constituents, in 1868, he said :—" I beg to thank you most cordially for the kind way in which you have returned me for the seventh time as your representative in Parliament. It is a position which for

D

more than a century and a half has been the most prized
distinction of my family: it was preferred by my great-
grandfather to an earldom, by my father to an earldom,
by myself to a peerage." The earldom was offered to
the late Sir Watkin after his return from the Peninsular
War, and he had so far entertained the idea as to fix on
the title, "Earl of Merioneth," if he grasped the prize.
Whether the present Sir Watkin would have accepted
the higher rank we are not in a position to say ; when the
peerage was offered him in 1859 he was on his way from
yachting in the Mediterranean, and upon his return,
Mr. W. W. E. Wynne, then member for Merioneth, communicated the intelligence to him, but Sir Watkin told
the late Lord Derby, the prime minister, that he would
not accept anything less than had been offered to
his father, to which his Lordship replied that he was
not of the same mind as Sir Charles Morgan (who was
raised to the peerage at the time), and there the matter
ended.

The principal entrance to Wynnstay is the one at
Rhuabon, and almost as soon as we enter the gates there
lies before us a beautiful avenue of more than a mile in
length, the first part of which is on level ground; then
comes a steep incline. This causes a singular optical
illusion, for, stand at which end you will, the other seems
to ascend. "Sir John Wynn's Oak," to the left of it, is
said to be one of the largest in the kingdom, the measure-
ment being as follows :—five feet from the ground, 27 ft.
8 in. in circumference ; eighteen inches from the ground,
36 ft. 1 in.; at the ground, 54 ft. Under its branches,
soon after the fire of 1858, a Bible, valued at a hundred
guineas, was presented to Lady Williams Wynn in the
presence of many thousands of people—a mark of the

sympathy of their neighbours with the family on the occasion of the disastrous fire. But visitors who roam about Wynnstay Park leave the avenue to the left, and turn up the path to the right, over a rustic bridge, through what are called "The Bath Grounds," and there the scene is one of fairyland. When the bath that gives the grounds their name is passed, there stands the Doric column, a hundred feet high, we have already mentioned, erected as a tribute of maternal affection to the memory of the second Sir Watkin Wynn. Visitors are allowed to climb the spiral staircase to its summit, where on a clear day the view is fine ; but Bingley, amongst others, expected too much, for he says "the prospect was sufficiently extensive, but in no degree interesting." Outside the Bath grounds, to the east, there is another notable oak, 17 ft. 10 in. round, at five feet from the ground; and unlike the other one it is so far scarcely decayed. An opinion has been expressed, however, to the effect that another half century will cause sad havoc to the foliage of Wynnstay Park, if the coal field is much further developed.

On leaving the Bath grounds the house immediately appears in sight, with its little lake in front and the deer, red and fallow, on the green sward ; and a further walk of a couple of miles will be found worth the labour. Even Mr. Bingley, who saw nothing to repay him for ascending the obelisk, was impressed with the beauty of the prospect from Nant y Belan. He says, " The ' Dingle of the Martin,' within the grounds of Wynnstay, is a deep and wooded hollow. The sides are precipitous and rocky, and the waters of the Dee, which roll along the bottom, are blackened by the shady banks, and for the most part concealed from the eye of the observer by the thickness of the foliage.

In the distant background I observed Chirk Castle, and the country round it, clad in lively colours, whilst, to the westward, I had a view of Castell Dinas Brân, crowning the summit of its steep. The whole vale of Llangollen, as far as the town, lay nearly in a straight line, and was richly varied with wood, rock, and pasture. The scene was closed in the horizon by the far distant British Alps, which bounded the sight." Bingley wrote towards the end of the last century, and we in this age have a bit of vantage ground that he did not possess. Whilst he was writing Sir Watkin and his " Ancient British Fencibles" were fighting our battles in Ireland, and, after the regiment was disbanded in 1800, Sir Watkin built Nant y Belan Tower—a classic mausoleum, in commemoration of the suppression of the Irish Rebellion. The names of those who fell are recorded in the cenotaph, and to these have been more recently added that of Captain Arthur W. Williams Wynn, of the Welsh Fusiliers, one of the heroes of the Alma.

And here our sketch must end. Our fathers, when they were lucky enough to " see the world " by a trip on the Rhine, were too much in the habit of depreciating home scenery on their return ; but in this age, when a run on the Rhine banks is an every day affair, we can afford to treat Welsh beauties more fairly ; and we are sure our friends will think with us that Lord Hanmer only did the Dee justice when he said—

"By the Elbe and through Rhineland I've wandered far and wide,
And by the Save, with silver tones, proud Danube's queenly bride,
By Arno's banks and Tiber's shore—but never did I see
A river I could match with thine, old Druid-haunted Dee."

NANT-Y-BELAN, AND VALE OF LLANGOLLEN.

BIRTH OF SIR WATKIN WILLIAMS WYNN.

THE *Cambro-Briton* of June 1820, contained an "Impromptu on the Birth of an Heir to the House of Wynnstay," and we cannot do better than reproduce the Welcome then given by the editor of the leading serial of educated Welshmen of the period to the "little stranger," who, we are most happy to say, has lived to realize the aspirations of the poet:

> Welcome, stranger, to our land,
>   Welcome to each hill and vale,
> Where the sons of Cymru stand,
>   Eager thy approach to hail.
>
> Joy and gladness for thee wait,
>   Honour too and love attend;
> In return be this thy fate,
>   Ever live old Cymru's friend.

A sneering Saxon critic a few years ago said that no Welshman seemed to be able to write verses about his country without putting the word "vales" into them to rhyme with "Wales;" but here we have a sample in disproof of the critic, although it must be confessed our poet has only just escaped! We insert the lines not for any beauty they possess, but as showing a pretty accurate estimate of the feeling of Welshmen generally to the House of Wynnstay, the head of which was then President of the Metropolitan Cambrian Institution, and a prominent supporter of every movement that had for its object the well-being of Welshmen.

Half a century ago the conveyance of news was as slow a process as that of any other commodity; so it was some days before Wales, generally, knew that an heir was born; for Sir Watkin, though he has developed into so true a Welshman, first saw the light in England, as the following announcement of his birth from the newspapers will shew:—

On Monday, May 22, 1820, at the house of Sir Watkin Williams Wynn, Bart., in Saint James's Square, London, Lady Harriet Williams Wynn of a son and heir.

Rhuabon had the first intimation, and that on the second day after
the event, and we are told, that "when the news reached Rhuabon on
the 24th the stores of the cellar and larder at Wynnstay were bountifully dispensed to the neighbouring poor, and the Festivities continued
throughout the week."

Half a century ago, too, penny-a-lining was, like Sir Watkin, in
its infancy, and the whole of the records of the various demonstrations
up and down the country did not occupy so much space in the newspapers as the report of the speeches at one dinner would in the
present "enlightened age."   We have said how the news was received
at Rhuabon, and we are told that on its way thither it set the bells
ringing at Shrewsbury and Oswestry; and we will now, in as concise
a manner as possible, show what followed the preliminary peals, in the
shape of gifts to the poor and feastings to the rich.   Ruthin led the
way with a meeting "called by the Aldermen," on May 31, in the
Town Hall, when a large number of the burgesses "drank the health
of Lady Harriet and her infant son."   Mr. Williams, of Plas-y-ward,
sent materials for a bon-fire, which was lighted up at night; fat sheep
were roasted, and served hot and wholesale to the poor; two barrels of
ale found ready customers, and when the bell-ringers paused to breathe,
a lusty band of musicians did not spare their wind.   On the day next but
one following, Mr. Williams entertained a party at dinner at his house,
in honour of the occasion, and after dinner a harper who was in
attendance most appropriately commemorated the birth by playing
"Sir Watkin's Delight."

There is always, necessarily, a good deal of sameness in demonstrations marking events of this character, but to make our record
complete we must, at least, name all the places, that we know of,
where something was done.   During the remaining days of May and
the early weeks of June commemorations were pretty general.   Thus,
Machynlleth "was brilliantly illuminated" and several sheep were
distributed amongst the poor.   At Wrexham there was a public dinner
and the poor were remembered bountifully.   There were "Festivities"
on a large scale on Llangedwyn Green.   At Llanfyllin there was a
dinner and distribution of meat.   Sir John Williams, of Bodelwyddan,
did honour to his young kinsman by "firing a royal salute in his park,"
and giving ale to all comers.   A bon-fire on the Green followed a
dinner and distribution at Llandrillo.   "C. Williams, Esq., presided
over a dinner at The Hand, Chirk," at which the guests numbered
more than a hundred.   Llwydiarth contented itself with providing good
things for the poor.   At Meifod and at Llanrhaiadr the House of

Powis divided the honours with that of Wynnstay, as was fitting in
Montgomeryshire, seeing that the young heir was so closely connected
with the family of Clive.   At the former place Mr J. Mytton, jun., and
Mr. Roberts, Groes, were the presidents.   At Bala the "guests at the
grand banquet" mustered to the number of two hundred, with
" R. W. Price, Esq., of Rhiwlas, and David Anwyl, Esq.," doing duty
as "chairman and vice."   At Llanrwst and Eglwysfach the festivities
were kept up for a couple of days ; the former place was for once rendered lively by the illuminations its inhabitants accomplished ; and the
beautiful valley that draws tourists to that locality was made gay after
dark by a huge bon-fire on Carreg-glen which "commanded the
general admiration of nearly the whole Vale of Conway."

With a couple more records our list is exhausted, although we
fear want of information has caused us to omit some places where the
birth of Sir Watkin was commemorated.   At Rhuabon a "hundred
and twenty gentlemen, freeholders, and friends of the House of
Wynnstay, dined ; E. L. Rowland, Esq. (in the absence of E. Youde,
Esq.) and Mr. Rowlands, of Pentreclawdd, presiding."   And at
Oswestry the dinner took place at the hotel, which in those days was
beginning to be called the " Wynnstay Arms," having previously been
more generally known as the " Eagles," " The Green," or the " Cross
Foxes."   The president at this dinner was "R. Salisbury, Esq.,
Deputy Mayor."   Before the Municipal Corporations' Act was passed,
it will be remembered, the chief magistrate himself was elected more
for ornament than for use ; but on a special occasion like this,
doubtless the Mayor would have been at the head of the table, had the
office that year not been filled by one of the Wynn family.   He was
then " Henry Watkin Williams Wynn, Esq.," but afterwards " Sir
Henry," and our Ambassador at Copenhagen ; and still later the father-
in-law of the young gentleman who was the active cause of all the
rejoicings we have recorded.   But to return to the Oswestry dinner.
Passing over what the record says of the good things provided, " which
seemed to set Epicurean invention at defiance," we will give one or two
of the toasts which do not seem to run in the stereotyped groove, as
for instance, " The Land we live in, and may those that don't like it
leave it ;" " Speed the Plough, and may Agriculture and Commerce go
hand in hand ;" and we will conclude our notice of the Birth-day
Festivities with the Toast of the Evening at Oswestry ; " The young
Heir-apparent to Wynnstay—may he live to emulate the courage of
his father and the virtues of his family, and to preserve the good old
stock of Ancient Britons."

ENGLYNION

A gyfansoddwyd ar yr achlysur gorfoleddus o

ENEDIGAETH MAB AC ETIFEDD

I'r clodfawr a'r enwog Wron,

Syr WATKIN WILLIAMS WYNN, Marchog.

———

Gwened holl feibion Gwynedd,—am eni
   Dymunawl Etifedd,
   I SYR WATKIN iesin wedd,
   Wr enwog, mawr ei rinwedd.

Fel yr haul, araul eirian,—O, coded
   Y cu-deg hardd faban,
   Fynu o'i gryd, gloyw-bryd glân,
   Yn hydr, i ddynawl oedran.

· Pwy Frython, o fron yn ddifrad,—na rydd
   Yn rhwyddwych dderchafiad,
   Teilwng heb un attaliad,
   I'r baban, mwynlan a mâd ?

Mae'n GYMRO drwyddo, o drâs,—y cedyrn
   Fu yn cadw ein teyrnas,
   'N galonog, rhag galanas
   'R hen elynion, coegion, câs.

Mewn iechyd o hyd, a hedd,—y byddo
   'R Mab addien yn Ngwynedd ;
   Yn ganwyll mewn gogonedd,
   Fel ei Dâd boed fâd hyd fedd.

                                MYLLIN.

VISIT OF THE PRINCESS VICTORIA TO WYNNSTAY.

WHEN Sir Watkin was twelve years of age, his father entertained at Wynnstay a no less distinguished visitor than the Princess Victoria, now our Most Gracious Queen.   The Princess and the Duchess of Kent, her mother, were on their way to Plas Newydd, Anglesea, in the early autumn of 1832, and paid visits, en route, to Powis Castle and Wynnstay.   At Shrewsbury their Royal Highnesses were met by Viscount Clive and the Hon. Robert Clive, the High Sheriff, Sir Rowland Hill, W. Ormsby Gore, Esq., and the Mayor and Corporation, and they lunched at the Talbot Hotel.   An address and a box of "Shrewsbury Cakes" having been duly presented, the Royal guests departed for Montgomeryshire; they were met on the confines of the county by a detachment of Yeomanry Cavalry, commanded by Captain Corrie.   The town of Welshpool was gaily decorated, and a large party of Poolonians of all grades welcomed the Princess and her Mother at Buttington, and escorted them through the town to Powis Castle.

The next afternoon the Royal tourists left for Wynnstay, arriving at Oswestry about four o'clock.   They were met at Llanymynech by the Oswestry squadron of the North Shropshire Yeomanry, commanded by Captain Croxon, and it is said that so anxious were the Borderers to see their future Queen, that the road all the way through Pant, Sweeney, and Morda was lined with spectators.   The ex-Mayor (in the absence of the Mayor, who had doubtless more important duties to perform!) and several of the leading members of the Corporation—including the Steward, the Hon. Thomas Kenyon—met the Royal party at Croeswylan gate, accompanied, of course, by a multitude of the townsfolk.   An address had been prepared, but "an express had been sent the previous evening to the Deputy-Mayor (Dr. Donne) from Powis Castle, to say that Her Royal Highness could not vary from her usual practice in not receiving addresses from places where she did not stop."   The Steward, however, was equal to the occasion; for, while the carriage stopped at the door of the Wynnstay Arms Hotel,

E

for the purpose of changing horses, " the Hon. T. Kenyon congratulated the Royal visitors in the name of the Corporation, and was commanded by the Duchess to inform the good people of Oswestry of the very great satisfaction she felt at the manner in which they were received by the inhabitants of the town and neighbourhood." And a memento of the borough was presented, which etiquette did not forbid, in the shape of the *History of Oswestry*, by the Rev. Peter Roberts and R. Minshull, which was accepted, and from this circumstance arose a signboard, novel in the town, to wit that of the Royal Arms over the door of Mr. Price, the publisher of the book.

At Chirk the party was met by the Denbighshire Yeomanry, accompanied by Sir Watkin, " in his splendid uniform of aide-de-camp to the King." And here it can be explained why the Mayor of Oswestry was not at the head of the Corporation to do the honours of his borough. It so happened that the Mayor was Sir Watkin himself, and so, not being able to be in two places at once, he naturally chose the more important one, and welcomed his illustrious guests on the border of his own county, to escort them to his mansion, where they were to rest. " The roar of cannon from the Castle announced the arrival at Chirk, which place they passed through, greeted by the villagers. The scene at the bridge was very imposing ; the two bodies of cavalry meeting on the confines of England and Wales ; the concourse of people ; the bright sunshine flashing on the swords and helmets of the Yeomanry, presented a spectacle not easily to be forgotten. At Newbridge a royal salute was fired by the staff of the Militia, as the party proceeded through the new entrance to Wynnstay Park."

There are those living at Rhuabon who remember the Saturday on which the Princess Victoria arrived at Wynnstay, and the enormous crowd of people who thronged the park as Her Royal Highness did so. And we have been told that, after the guests were safely housed, a horse in one of the carriages, growing restive, ran away amongst the people, maiming several before it could be controlled.

Space will fail us to record in detail how the Royal party attended the Parish Church of Rhuabon on the Sunday, when the service was performed by the Rev. Rowland Wingfield, doubtless to an overflowing congregation. Or how on Monday the Pontcysyllte Aqueduct was visited, and admired, and how, when Wynnstay was finally left, and horses were changed at the " King's Head," Llangollen, the name of that hotel was changed, too, into the " Royal Hotel." Having accompanied the party so far, it is no part of our work to trace further the Royal Progress into Wales.

COMING-OF-AGE OF SIR WATKIN.

THIS important event in the life of the Baronet was duly honoured throughout a large district in North Wales and the Borders. The two most extensive demonstrations were those of Wrexham and Oswestry in May, 1841; and in the following September the coming-of-age was celebrated at Wynnstay by a week's festivities, which included a visit from Sir Watkin to Oswestry to take part in an important ceremony, and the reception of a deputation from Wrexham.

During the week commencing September 6th, 1841, Wynnstay was full of guests, including the Duke and Duchess of Northumberland, the Duke of Marlborough, Lord and Lady Delamere, Rt. Hon. C. W. W. Wynn, M.P., and family, Lady C. Stewart, Sir P. and Lady Egerton, Sir S. Glynne, Sir Rowland Hill, Sir J. Williams, Hon. Mr. Bagot.

At Brynkinalt, Viscount Dungannon entertained the Marquis and Marchioness of Londonderry, Lord Castlereagh, Countess of Jersey, and Lady Clementina Villiars.

A pavilion was erected at Wynnstay, capable of dining 600 persons, and communicating with the mansion by a corridor joining the window of the drawing room, which on this occasion was used as a ball room. Collinet's band from London, including Herr Koenig and his cornet-a-piston, was engaged for the week, and Gunters looked after the refreshments. On a raised side-board in the pavilion were placed the old plate and other heir-looms of the family, including the rich and magnificent vase presented to the late Sir Watkin by the nobility, gentry and clergy of Denbighshire, in 1816, as a token of the respect in which he was held.

Although the celebration was adjourned to September, the birthday was in one way marked in May, viz., by the drawing of four hogsheads of ale, brewed by Mr. Martin on the occasion of Sir Watkin's birth, and thirty hogsheads of other fine taps. In the celebrations of September four more hogsheads of birth-day ale were drunk, and it is said that 200 measures of malt had been consumed to brew the ale on the occasion of Sir Watkin's birth, and this was all disposed of at the coming-of-age.

The festivities of the week commenced with a family dinner-party of sixty on Monday; and on Tuesday there was a grand ball, open to 500 or 600 guests from all quarters. Sir Watkin and the Duchess of Northumberland led off the ball, followed by the Hon. Hugh Cholmondeley and Miss Williams Wynn.

On Wednesday a deputation from Wrexham was received, introduced by Sir William Lloyd, Knight; Mr. Lewis read an address, and Mr. Rowland presented it. Mr. Lewis, after reading the address, repeated the following Druidical prophecy:—

> " Dywad Derwyddon
> Dadeni Haelon
> O Hil Eryron o'r Eryri,"

and expressed a wish that it might be fulfilled in Sir Watkin's person.

On Wednesday evening there was a grand banquet, and after dinner a subscription was made for the colliers of the neighbourhood who, at the time, were in distress owing to the badness of trade.

The rest of the week was employed in banquets, dinners, and sports. On Saturday the poorer folk had a dinner in the pavilion, and the week closed with a grand display of fireworks.

At Oswestry the authorities killed two birds with one stone—that is to say they fêted Sir Watkin and laid the foundation-stone of the Cross Market Hall on the same day, viz. Monday, Sept. 13, 1841. Mr. Penson was the Mayor, and the town was gaily decorated; the weather was delightful, and there was a general holiday. At noon Sir Watkin entered the town—four-in-hand, and he was welcomed at the Wynnstay Hotel by the Odd-Fellows. He then proceeded to the Mayor's house, where he was met by his worship, attended by the Hon. T. Kenyon, Sir John Hanmer, Dr. Donne, &c., &c. The Earl of Powis shortly afterwards arrived, accompanied by the Hon. E. H. Clive. At 1 o'clock, a large procession accompanied Sir Watkin to the Guildhall, where an address was presented to the young baronet, and Sir Watkin made a suitable reply. The procession then re-formed, and the mayor and corporation escorted the Earl of Powis and party to the Cross, when the Earl laid the first stone of the Market Hall. Here the ceremonies partook of congratulation to Sir Watkin as well as to the town, and the speeches by the Earl, the Hon. E. H. Clive, Hon. T. Kenyon, and the Mayor referred to the two events. After the ceremonies the Mayor gave a lunch on his lawn, of which 200 partook. We should say that the Duke of Northumberland took part in the proceedings of the day. There was a ball at the Wynnstay Arms at night.

The Coming-of-age of "Sir John Barleycorn," the monster cask brewed when Sir Watkin was born, and tapped when he came of age, shares the honours with the baronet in the following :—

THE WYNNSTAY ALE.

All hail to the honor of nut-brown October;
  We'll drink it and praise it, no further perplext :
When preaching men go into clubs to keep sober,
  The sermon's oft brandy, though water's the text.
    At dinner or luncheon,
    The pump and the puncheon,
By half-and-half taking it, put them at par;
    So if you'll thus fix it,
    And equally mix it,
'Twill keep us at peace, and uphold us in war!

Rally all wine-bibbers, steady and *dryly*,
  The ruby grape rescue from slander and jeer;
They tell us the d——l has bottled up slyly
  All felon vices in brandy and beer.
    All hail two-bottle men,
    Not quite tee-tottle men,
For storm cloud of cannon, or grog smok'd cigar :
    If Old England sought her men
    All among water-men,
Woe to our banner in peace or in war!

Let's drink to Sir John Barleycorn Wynn in a bumper,
  A native of Wynnstay, a *baronet* sage;
In his earliest days he was always a thumper,
  Like master like man—he has just come of age.
    From the same year though sprung,
    One's old and one's young;
One's train'd for the army, and one for the bar!
    But spur him anon,
    There's much fight in Sir John!
Though merry in peace, he's a hero in war.

Of beef and of beer we have all had our rations;
  Fam'd baronets both are—Sir Watkin ; Sir John ;
(A branch call'd small beer are Sir John's poor relations,
  In seasons so jolly look'd little upon.)
    As baronet's brother,
    Drink one in the other,
Fit stingo for soldiers, a grog for a tar;
    May fate never press him—
    "Sir Watkin; God Bless Him!"
Our Ring Dove in peace, and our Eagle in War.

THE COMING-OF-AGE AT OSWESTRY.

SOMETIMES the placards hung out at newspaper offices pur-
porting to give the contents of the paper sold within are said to
be richer in news than the prints themselves, but this, of course, is a
libel. Not so, however, as regards the bills, many yards long, in which
it used to be the custom to announce Festivities connected with
Coming-of-Ages and the like:—no mere newspaper report of the proceedings could convey the same idea that these wonderful productions
produced in the reader! We give two—Oswestry and Wrexham—
issued in 1841, when the present Sir Watkin came of age. Of course
we cannot pretend to the glories of type displayed in the programmes.

OSWESTRY.

THE

COMING-OF-AGE OF

SIR

W. W. WYNN, BART.,

Will be celebrated in Oswestry by

TWO DAYS' FESTIVITIES,

Expressive of the strong Attachment of the
Inhabitants of the Town and Neighbourhood to the

FAMILY OF WYNNSTAY.

On Saturday, May 22nd, 1841,

The day on which Sir W. W. Wynn, Bart.,
attains his Majority,

A GRAND

PUBLIC DINNER

Will take place at the

WYNNSTAY ARMS INN,

In a large

PAVILION

Erected on the Green, capable of accom-
modating

500 PERSONS.

President:—

William Ormsby Gore, Esq., M.P.

Vice-Presidents:—

The Honourable Thomas Kenyon,
Sir John Roger Kynaston, Bart.,
Thomas Penson, Esq., Mayor.
John Ralph Ormsby Gore, Esq., M.P.,
William Lloyd, Esq., Aston,
Thomas Netherton Parker, Esq.
Joseph Venables Lovett, Esq.,
Thomas Lovett, Esq.,
John Jones, Esq., Brook Street,
John Croxon, Esq.,
W. W. E. Wynne, Esq., Ruyton Hall,
H. P. Tozer Aubrey, Esq.,
R. H. Kinchant, Esq.

Dinner Ticket, 7s., including Ale and
Dessert.

Dinner on the Table precisely at 3 p.m.

AN EARLY APPLICATION
For Tickets is requested to be made at the
Bar of the Wynnstay Arms Inn, where
gentlemen intending to dine will be kind
enough to leave their names.

THE
PAVILION
Will be handsomely decorated with *Drapery*
and appropriate *Devices*, and the *Arms* of
Wynnstay emblazoned on a large *Trans-
parency* opposite the Chair.   Over the
Chair will be constructed a Canopy or Arch
with a

TRANSPARENT INSCRIPTION,
And the whole building will be

BRILLIANTLY ILLUMINATED WITH GAS, IN
FANCY LAMPS,
And Chandeliers, under the able management of Mr. Roberts, Gas Proprietor.   On
the outside a

LARGE FLAG,
With the Cross Foxes and Spread Eagles,
will float from the Gable, under which will
appear Sir Watkin's Initials in *Coloured
Lamps*, interspersed with Laurel, &c.

THE
PROCESSION
Will form at the Wynnstay Arms, at 8
o'clock in the Morning, which will be

ANNOUNCED BY THE FIRING OF CANNON

From the Castle Hill, and the

RINGING OF THE BELLS

Of the Old Church.

A Splendid
UNION JACK
Will float from the Steeple, presented to
the Town in honour of the occasion.

THE BAND OF THE NORTH SHROPSHIRE
YEOMANRY
Will lead the Procession ;

BELLMAN, ON HORSEBACK ;
FLAGS AND BANNERS
Emblematic of the Birthday, and of the
Attachment of the Town and Neighbour-
hood to

Sir WATKIN WILLIAMS WYNN, Bt.
FIRST OX,
On a Waggon, drawn by Four Grey Horses.
SECOND OX,
Drawn by Four Grey Waggon Horses.
THIRD OX,
Drawn by Four Grey Waggon Horses.
FOURTH OX,
Drawn by Four Grey Waggon Horses.
FIFTH OX,
Drawn by Four Grey Waggon Horses.
Master Butchers—Messrs. Poole and Lewis,
Attendants, &c.

COMMITTEE OF MANAGEMENT,
In Carriages :—

GENTRY, TENANTRY, AND TRADESMEN :—

THE DIFFERENT CLUBS

Who may wish to attend ; at the head of
which will be

THE SPIRITED ASSOCIATION OF
ODD FELLOWS,
Preceded by a
FIRST-RATE BAND,
The Different Grades of the Order parading
with their distinctive Decorations and
Embellishments :—

The Rest of the Inhabitants in Regular
Order.
WITH FLAGS, &c.

THE PROCESSION
Will advance from
THE WYNNSTAY ARMS,
To the Cross and up Bailey Street, to the
Guildhall Square, where a Halt will take
place :—the Bands playing

"SIR WATKIN'S DELIGHT"
With Nine Times Nine.
The Procession will then pass along Leg
Street, to the Cross, and up Church Street,
to the Wynnstay Arms, when
NINE TIMES NINE WILL AGAIN BE GIVEN :
It will then advance
Along Church Street, and down Lower
Brook Street, and enter the Lower Yard
of the Wynnstay Arms, where the

SPLENDID OXEN WILL BE DISTRIBUTED TO THE POOR OF THE TOWN AND SURROUNDING NEIGHBOURHOOD.

The Procession will then pass on

TO THE MAESYLLAN.

RURAL SPORTS
AND PASTIMES
IN THE MAESYLLAN.

The Divers Games and Pastimes, in order as hereinafter set forth, will come off on *Saturday, May 22nd*, in the Field at Maesyllan, the Gates of which will be opened at Eight o'clock in the Morning. The Sports will be commenced precisely at Ten, and the Competition for the Prizes shall be open to all comers, under the Conditions after mentioned.

Stewards of the Sports and Pastimes :—
  Mr. Robert Roberts, Salop Road,
  Mr. Gough, Upper Brook Street.
Judge, Mr. Hammond.

1.—The Wynnstay Stakes—A Pony Race, for Ponies of Thirteen hands and under, for a Purse of 2 Sovereigns. Entrance 1s., to go to the Second Horse, with 5s. added by the Fund. Best of Heats. Mile Course. Any former winner to be weighted accordingly.

2.—Jingling Match for 5s , and 2s 6d. to the Jingler.

3.—First Donkey Race for 10s. The Second Donkey to receive 2s. 6d. Straight Race. No Whippers in. Heats.

4.—Wheelbarrow Race for 5s. The Candidates to Run Blindfold, and to turn round three times.

5.—Foot Race for Men. 5s, the first, and 2s. 6d. the second.

6.—The Maesyllan Stakes. For Ponies not exceeding twelve hands. A Purse of £2. Entrance 1s. each, to go to the Second Horse, with 5s. added. The Ponies to be entered at the Wynnstay Arms on Friday evening at 6 o'clock.

7.—Bag Race for 2s. 6d. Heats. Distance 50 yards.

8.—Grinning through a Collar for 2s. 6d. Heats.

9.—Climbing the Pole for various Prizes, viz., a Leg of Mutton, a New Hat. and a Pair of Shoes.

10.—Second Donkey Race for 5s. the First, and 2s. 6d. the Second. To be ridden by Sweeps with Brushes. Heats.

11.—Ladies' Race for a Pound of Tea.

12.—Contest for Hasty Pudding for a Prize of 2s. 6d., *including Pudding.* Hasty Pudding and 2-pronged Forks to be provided. The Prize to be given to the Fastest Eater and Cleanest Finisher.

13.—Race on All Fours for 5s. Distance 50 yards.

14.—Third Donkey Race for 10s., the First, and 2s. 6d. the Second. No one to ride his own Donkey. The Donkey last in to be winner of the Heat. Best of Heats.

15.—Hurdle Race for 5s. the First, and 2s. 6d. the Second.

16.—Race for a Porker. Any one attempting to catch the Porker by the ears or legs, or in any other way save and except by the Tail only ; and any one who shall take the Tail in his teeth and use any unfa r advantage, shall subject himself to ejectment from the lists.

17.—Grand Donkey Tournament and Presage of Broomstails on Donkeys, for 5s.
  1. Each combatant must come to the ground provided with a Hearth Broom, not more than five nor less than four-and-a-half feet in length.
  2. No Knight undonkeyed in any fair charge, to enjoy the privilege of a second encounter.
  3. Any Knight who shall have recourse to assault and battery with his Lance, otherwise called Broadsword Exercise, shall be pronounced a Craven, and forthwith ejected from the lists.
  4. The Acts and Deeds of all refractory Donkeys to be at the sole risk of their riders.

18.—Race for a New Gown, Distance 50 yards.

19.—Bobbing for Rolls and Treacle for 2s. 6d.

20.—Grand Foot Steeple Chase for 10s.

FINALE,
A Grand
PROMENADE
Of all the Characters
ROUND THE FIELD
In the following order, to wit.
1
THE BELLMAN
REVERSED ON HIS CHARGER.
2
THE WINNING DONKEYS,
Led by their Riders.
3
THE CONQUEROR
Of the Lists, Mounted.
4
THE SUCCESSFUL COMPETITORS
Of the other Prizes.
5
BAND
Playing.
6
THE GENTLEMEN FORMING THE
COMMITTEE
OF MANAGEMENT.
Completing the Circle of the Field the
Stewards shall propose
HEALTH, WEALTH,
LONG LIFE,
AND HAPPINESS TO
SIR WATKIN.

No Horses or Donkeys besides those
intended for the Races to be admitted
within the Gates, and those admitted must
be led, not ridden. A Ribbon shall be given
to each winner of a Prize, and worn round
the arm. No winner of one race shall be
allowed to start for another.

———o———

SECOND DAY'S FESTIVITIES,
Wednesday, May 26th.

———

A RURAL FETE
Will take place
ON THE GREEN OF THE
WYNNSTAY ARMS,
In the evening of the 22nd of May; for
which occasion

AN EXCELLENT BAND
Has been engaged.
DANCING
To commence at half-past 4.
TEA
Will be provided for the Company.

At half-past 9, a
MAGNIFICENT DISPLAY
OF
FIRE WORKS
Will be exhibited in
THE MAESYLLAN,
Under the superintendence of
MR. J. G. D'ERNST,
Artist in Fire Works to Her Majesty, and
the Vauxhall Gardens,
Dancing will be resumed in the
PAVILION
Which, as well as
THE GREEN,
Will be
BRILLIANTLY ILLUMINATED
For the occasion.

Negus and Refreshments provided for
the Company. Gentlemen's Tickets, 2s.;
Ladies' Tickets, 1s. each.

The whole of the
ARRANGEMENTS
Will be conducted in such a manner as to
ensure to all those who participate in the
RECREATIONS OF THE DAY
A most pleasing remembrance of
THE FETE
In Honour of the Coming-of-Age of
SIR WATKIN WILLIAMS WYNN,
Baronet.
By order of the Committee of Management.

———

W. Price, Printer, Oswestry.

F

THE WREXHAM PROGRAMME.

THE Wrexham Programme is even more elaborate than the Oswestry one, and will prove interesting to readers in that district :—

CELEBRATION

OF THE

COMING-OF-AGE

OF

SIR W. W. WYNN, BART.,

AT WREXHAM,

1841.

——

Saturday, the 22nd of May,

THE ANNIVERSARY

OF THE

BARONET'S BIRTHDAY

Will be ushered in by ringing the Bells.

A FLAG,

Emblazoned with the

ARMS OF THE HOUSE OF WYNNSTAY,

Will be displayed from one of the Turrets of the Steeple, and remain to the conclusion of the Festivities.

At Noon,

A SALUTE OF TWENTY-ONE ROUNDS

OF

CANNON

(Kindly lent for the occasion by Simon Yorke, Esq.)

WILL BE FIRED.

The Bells will Ring throughout the Day.

——

Monday, May the 24th,

Will be observed as a

GENERAL HOLIDAY;

The Bells will Ring throughout the Day.

At 11 o'clock a.m.,

A

PROCESSION

Will be formed in the Ruthin Road in the following order :—

TWO TRUMPETERS,

TWO MARSHALLS ON HORSEBACK,

A Detachment of the

DENBIGHSHIRE YEOMANRY CAVALRY.

BAND,

MR. R. JOHNSON'S WAGGON,

Drawn by 3 Horses, decorated with green and red favors, containing an

OX AND 8 SHEEP,

MR. JOHNSON'S (SECOND)

Waggon and 3 Horses, decorated as above, containing an

OX AND 8 SHEEP,

MRS. DAVIES'S (LLWYNKNOTIA)

Waggon and 3 Horses, decorated as above, containing an

OX AND 8 SHEEP,

MR. J. HARRISON'S (PLAS-COCH)

Waggon and 3 Horses, decorated as above, containing an

The Procession at Wrexham. 43

OX AND 8 SHEEP,

Mr. J. Birch's (Gwersyllt)

Waggon and 3 Horses, decorated as above, containing an

OX AND 8 SHEEP.

(The above Oxen are the munificent gift of Sir Watkin, placed at the disposal of the Committee for the Poor of Wrexham, Marchwiel, and Gwersyllt.)

BOYS

Of the various Day Schools in the Town, under the superintendence of their respective Teachers ;

MEMBERS

Of the various

TEMPERANCE SOCIETIES

Of the Town and Neighbourhood ;

FRIENDLY SOCIETIES,

Accompanied by the various Banners and Flags belonging to each Society, in the following order :—

The King's Head Society,
Ivorites,
Ancient Britons' Friendly Society,
The Waterloo Society,
The Friendly Union Society,
(Fleece Inn)
The United Society,
The Amicable Society,
The Union Society,
The Senior Society,

And other Societies in order of seniority, Various Lodges of the

Loyal and Independent Order of

ODD FELLOWS,

With their Regalia, Ensigns, Flags, and Banners.

LARGE BANNER ;

Staff of the Royal Denbigh Militia,

BAND,

The

GENTRY, CLERGY,

And Inhabitants of the Town and Neighbourhood,

COACH

And Four Piebald Horses,

Belonging to Messrs. Jones and Herbert, of Chester, decorated with Green and Red Favors, Flags, &c.,

Containing Members of the Committee ;

COACH

And Four Grey Horses,

Belonging to Messrs. Jones and Herbert, of Chester, decorated with Green and Red Favors, Flags, &c.,

Containing Members of the Committee ;

COACH

And Four Piebald Horses,

Belonging to Mr. Smith, of Eastham, decorated with Green and Red Favors, Flags, &c.,

Containing Members of the Committee ;

COACH

And Four Bay Horses,

Belonging to Mr. Smith, of Eastham, decorated with Green and Red Favors, Flags, &c.,

Containing Members of the Committee ;

CARRIAGE

And Four Horses,

Belonging to Mr. R. Johnson, decorated with Green and Red Favors, Flags, &c.

CARRIAGE

And Four Horses,

Belonging to Mr. R. Johnson, decorated with Green and Red Favors, Flags, &c.

The Head of the Procession will be at the Bowling-Green Inn, and the various Waggons, Schools, Friendly Societies, Coaches, and other parties joining are to take the route from town up to Pentrefelin past Belle-Vue, and form in the places assigned in the Ruthin Road.

At 12 o'clock,

A SALUTE OF 21 CANNON

Will be Fired,

Immediately after which

THE PROCESSION

Will move through the Town

In the following route, viz. :

Pen-y-bryn, Town Hill, Hope Street, King Street, Lambpit Street, Chester Street, Yorke Street, Mount Street, Salop Street, Madeira Hill, Pen-y-bryn, Town Hill, High Street, Charles Street, to the Beast Market, where the assemblage will disperse; the Clubs

to their respective Houses; the Schools to
their several Rooms, and the Waggons with
Oxen and Sheep to the Queen Square.

At 5 o'clock,

A SERIES OF POPULAR

A M U S E M E N T S ,

Under the direction of the Committee, will
be provided.

At 9 o'clock, the

WYNNSTAY ARMS, TOWN HALL,
And the

CHURCH GATES

Will be

I L L U M I N A T E D

WITH APPROPRIATE DEVICES;

And a

GRAND DISPLAY

OF

F I R E W O R K S ,

Under the personal superintendence of

MR. JAMES,

Of the Gardens, Birkenhead, and the
Zoological Gardens, Liverpool,

. WILL BE GIVEN

IN HIGH STREET.

Tuesday, May the 25th,

THE BELLS WILL RING AS BEFORE,

THE CANNON WILL FIRE A SALUTE, AT NOON,
AS BEFORE.

A N   O X

Will be

R O A S T E D   W H O L E

IN THE BEAST MARKET,

And will afterwards be conveyed to Queen
Square, to be cut up for the Dinner on
Wednesday.

At 4 o'clock,

A   D I N N E R

Will take place

AT THE WYNNSTAY ARMS INN,

President :—

SIR R. H. CUNLIFFE, BT., C.B.

Vice-Presidents :—

Sir William Lloyd,
H. W. Meredith, Esq.,
R. M. Lloyd, Esq.,
Townshend Mainwaring, Esq.,
Simon Yorke, Esq.,
Capt. E. Jones,
John Foulkes, Esq.,
Thomas Edgworth, Esq.

Stewards :—

The Most Honourable the Marquis of
Westminster,
Viscount Dungannon,
The Hon. F. West,
The Hon. W. Bagot, M.P.
The Hon. E. Ll. Mostyn,
The Hon. Ll. Kenyon,
Sir S. R. Glynne, Bart., M.P.,
Col. Myddelton Biddulph,
Col. Wynne, Garthewin,
Thomas Fitzhugh, Esq.,
F. R. Price, Esq.,
P. P. Cooke, Esq.,
F. J. Hughes, Esq., M.D.,
C. B. T. Roper, Esq.,
J. Wynne Eyton, Esq.,
John Williams, Esq.,
Capt. Jones Parry, R.N.,
Dr. Phillips Jones,
T. Wynne Eyton, Esq.,

Tickets, 7s. each, to be had at the Bar of
the Wynnstay Arms.

A   B A N D ,

Under the direction of Mr. Hughes (late of
the Royal Denbigh Band), will be in
attendance, and a party of

GENTLEMEN AMATEURS,

Resident in Wrexham, have kindly
promised to

SING SEVERAL POPULAR GLEES AND SONGS

During the Evening.

On Wednesday, the 26th of May,

A   D I N N E R

Will be given in

HIGH STREET,

Under the superintendence of
Messrs. EDGWORTH, HUMPHREYS, RICHARDS, AND PAINTER,

TO 2000 PERSONS;

The Dinner will consist of the

OXEN AND SHEEP,

(Placed at the disposal of the Committee by Sir Watkin)

2000 LOAVES
Of Bread,
10 CWT.
OF

PLUM PUDDING
AND
6 HOGSHEADS
OF

ALE

Sent for the occasion
FROM THE CELLARS OF WYNNSTAY.

The Dinner will be laid on Twenty Tables. Each table will be distinguished by a number inscribed on a Flag; the odd numbers on Green Flags and the even ones on Red. Each table will also have a president and vice-president, and six carvers; and the Guests will be served by six attendants, and three persons will supply them with Ale.

The *Plates to be used* have been ordered by the Committee expressly for the occasion, and one will be given to each Guest. They will have an inscription in commemoration of the event, mounted on a shield borne by a Spread Eagle, bearing also the *Motto* of the *House of Wynnstay,* "Nec me meminisse pigebit."

No person will be admitted to the Dinner without a Ticket, which may be obtained from a Subscriber to the Fund. The Committee will forward Tickets to the resident Subscribers, and to the Agents of the non-residents, in proportion of Five to every Pound Subscribed.

The Company will assemble in the Beast Market at 1 o'clock. Each guest will see by his Ticket at which Table he must take his place; and he will also see by a corresponding Flag where his President is stationed

in the Beast Market: The Bearer will go to him and be under his direction. The Company will move in procession, headed by a Band, from the Market up Holt Street, Lambpit Street, and Hope Street, to High Street, at 2 o'clock.

SIR WILLIAM LLOYD
WILL PRESIDE,
And all Orders, Toasts, &c., will be given by him and will be repeated by the President at each Table. A full

MILITARY BAND
Will play a variety of beautiful airs during and after dinner.

After Dinner, the President will give "THE HEALTH OF THE QUEEN;" After which the Company will sing

"GOD SAVE THE QUEEN!"
Accompanied by the Band.
The Chairman will then give
"THE HEALTH OF SIR W. W. WYNN, AND MAY HE LONG LIVE AND ENJOY MANY HAPPY RETURNS OF THE DAY;"
After the Cheers have ceased the Band will play

"SIR WATKIN'S DELIGHT!"
At 5 o'clock the Band will proceed to the Beast Market, where they will be followed by the Company to participate in the various

AMUSEMENTS
Which will there be provided for them.

THE CHILDREN
Of the
VARIOUS DAY SCHOOLS
Will be provided with
TEA AND PLUM BREAD
At their Respective School Rooms, under the superintendence of their Teachers.

THE POOR
In the Workhouse will be regaled with
ROAST BEEF
AND
PLUM PUDDING.

Printed at the Jedburgh Press, by T. Painter, High Street, Wrexham.

SIR WATKIN AND THE FREEMASONS.

WHEN the Lodge of Saint Oswald was formed in Oswestry in 1866, the Brethren were fortunate enough to obtain from Sir Watkin some antique chairs and other furniture that had been formerly used in a Lodge holden at Wynnstay. At what precise date this Lodge met we have never been able to ascertain—but certainly it dates back as far as the time of the grandfather of the present baronet. If there were any records existing they probably shared the fate of other, and far more valuable documents, destroyed at the great fire of 1858.

In connection with the mystic art we have chiefly now to do with the present owner of Wynnstay. Sir Watkin was initiated into the mysteries of Freemasonry in the Cheshire Provence, over a quarter of a century ago, and in 1851 became Worshipful Master of the Cestrian Lodge, and he celebrated the event by inviting all his brethren there to a banquet at Wynnstay on the 14th July in that year. The Chester lodge at that time had belonging to it several eminent men as active members; notably the veteran hero Lord Combermere; Lord Chief Justice Jarvis; Mr. Welsby, Recorder of Chester; &c., and these names we find amongst those who accepted invitations to the dinner.

In 1852 Sir Watkin received the distinguished appointment he holds at the present time, that of Provincial Grand Master of North Wales and Shropshire. The Grand Lodge warrant appointing " our well-beloved Brother Sir Watkin Williams Wynn, in the County of Denbigh, baronet; Representative in Parliament for the County of Denbigh; Lieut.-Col. Commandant of the Montgomeryshire Yeomanry Cavalry, and Steward of Her Majesty's Manorial Courts in Denbigh-shire—*Provincial Grand Master* for North Wales, with the County of Salop added," is dated January 13, 1852, and is signed " Zetland, G.M.; Yarborough, D.G.M.; William H. White, G.S." The ceremony of Installation took place at Shrewsbury on the 9th of March, 1852, when " Bro. the Right Hon. Lord Combermere, the Hero of Bhurt-pore, the Right Worshipful the Grand Master for Cheshire, who had taken great interest in Sir Watkin's masonic movements, was specially

deputed by the Grand Master of England, Lord Zetland, to perform
the ceremony of Installation." Brother White, Grand Junior Deacon
of England, attended with the warrant of appointment, and the direction of the ceremonies devolved upon Bro. Griffiths, G.S. of the
Cheshire Provence, at Lord Combermere's request. The Rev. Canon
Bowles, D.P.G.M. for Herefordshire, acted as Deputy Grand Master,
and amongst the Brethren who assisted were Lord Dungannon, Sir
Andrew V. Corbet, the Rev. J. Osmond Dakeyne, one of the Grand
Chaplains of England, &c. Sir Watkin was introduced and presented
by Bro. Col. Burlton, *C.B.*, Grand Master for the Provence of Bengal.

The ceremony over, the newly-installed P.G.M. invested the
following brethren as his first officers :—

> Rev. E. H. Dymock, Deputy Grand Master.
> W. J. Clement, P.G. Senior Warden.
> J. N. Heathcote, P.G. Junior Warden.
> Thomas Onions, P.G. Registrar.
> Rev. J. G. Guise, P.G. Chaplain.
> Rev. P. G. Bentley, P.G. Chaplain.
> J. P. White, P.G. Treasurer.
> Charles Wigan, P.G. Secretary.
> Robert Pritchard, P.G. Senior Deacon.
> John Stevenson, P.G. Junior Deacon.
> H. T. Wace, P.G. Superintendent.
> J. L. Rowland, P.G. Director of Ceremonies.
> S. Wood, P.G. Assistant do.   do.
> J. Broughall, P.G. Swordbearer.
> Henry Bloxam, P.G. Organist.
> John Towers, P.G. Pursuivant.

A Banquet was held in the evening and Addresses were delivered
from various Lodges congratulating Sir Watkin on his appointment.

As all this will be read by outsiders we may just remark that what
are called the "Craft Lodges" the Provincial Grand Master was here
chosen to preside over have not been inaptly termed the House of
Commons of Freemasonry; and that there is a higher degree—or
House of Lords, in which 'Brethren' become 'Companions' and
'Lodges' are called 'Chapters.' And this is known as the "Royal
Arch." Sir Watkin did not solve the mysteries of this degree until after
he became the chief of the Blue and Purple Lodges. And to take it he
went to the county where he had taken his first lessons in the craft,
and on the 4th of April, 1853, at the Chapter connected with what was
then the Lodge of Fidelity of Birkenhead—and numbered 701 on the
Books of the Grand Chapter of England—the Provincial Grand Master

of North Wales and Salop passed under the Royal Arch. In 1859 he was appointed " Most Excellent Superintendent of the Provence," and the warrant of appointment is signed by " Zetland, Z., Panmure, H., J. H. Hall, J., Wm. Grey Clarke, E., and J. Llewellyn Evans, N." Under this warrant Sir Watkin presides over all the Grand Chapters of Shropshire and North Wales.

Before we leave the subject of Masonry we may remark that there have been few Provincial Grand Masters, if any, in rural provinces, who have performed so much masonic work as Sir Watkin has done. During the time he has been P.G.M. the following Lodges have been consecrated :—Admaston, June 16, 1852, (removed to Wellington in 1857); Ludlow, July 13, 1853 ; Carnarvon, August 8, 1854; Llandudno, 1858; Welshpool, March 31, 1864; Llangefni, Oct. 24, 1866; Oswestry (St. Oswalds) Nov. 5, 1866; Ironbridge, Nov. 27, 1866; Denbigh, Oct. 24, 1867; Wrexham, Mar. 14, 1871; Bala, May 3, 1872; Oswestry, (Fitzalan) June 21, 1873; Mold, Feb. 26, 1874; Amlwch, Sep. 3, 1874; and Portmadoc, Oct. 29, 1874. And, we may add, there is looming in the future still further work, in the consecration of Lodges at Market Drayton, Llanidloes, Newtown, Towyn, and probably other places.

In connection with Masonry, it is pleasant to record one act of the Brethren of the Provence when their Grand Master got married in 1852. On the 29th of April that year several of the most distinguished members commemorated the event by a dinner at Shrewsbury, Brother the Rev. E. H. Dymock and Brother W. J. Clement presiding.

With the further record of more public acts in connection with Freemasonry we conclude this portion of our subject. In 1864 the P.G.M. laid the Corner Stone of Trinity Church, Llandudno ; in 1867 he opened the Masonic Hall of the same town, and in 1869 he laid the Foundation Stone of the Oswestry Cottage Hospital.

LADY WILLIAMS WYNN.

MARRIAGE OF SIR WATKIN.

SIR WATKIN was married on the twenty-eighth of April, 1852, to his cousin, Miss Marie Emily Williams Wynn, daughter of the Right Hon. Sir Henry Williams Wynn, K.C.B., Her Majesty's Minister at the Court of Denmark. The ceremony took place in St. James's Church, London ; the Hon. and Rev. Henry Cholmondeley, second son of Lord Delamere, and cousin of the bridegroom, and the Rev. J. Jackson, rector of the parish, officiated. Our fair readers, who would naturally wish for a description of the costumes worn on the occasion, must pardon our declining to follow " Jenkins of the *Morning Post* " through his elaborate description of toilettes of the bridesmaids, and be content with a list of their names. They were the Hon. Cecilia Carington, Lady Harriet Herbert, Miss Somerset, the Hon. Lucy Neville, the Hon. Harriet Cholmondeley, and Miss Gaskell. The wedding breakfast took place at the residence of Lord Carington, uncle of the bride, covers being laid for seventy guests.

The demonstrations in North Wales and on the borders, following this event, were on a scale of unusual magnificence, and space would fail us to recount a tenth part of what was done during the merry month of May following. At Oswestry £240 was collected, and a committee formed, of which Mr. Peploe Cartwright was chosen chairman ; Mr. J. Miles Hales, secretary ; and Mr. Robert Williams, treasurer ; three well-known townsmen, who have long since passed away. The festivities lasted three days ; viz., May 3, when rural sports in Maesyllan, a grand procession, distribution of meat, &c., and a public dinner, "jumped with the humour " of various classes :— May 7, when Sir Watkin and his bride passed through the gaily-decorated town on their way to Welshpool ;—and May 11, when a rural fête was held in the Wynnstay Arms Green that has never been surpassed by anything of the kind in the annals of Oswestry. And before we leave Oswestry we should say that the school children were not forgotten ; those of the British Schools having a trip to Chirk, at

G

the expense of Mr. E. W. Thomas, The Cross, accompanied by Mr. Thomas Minshall, that year Mayor of Oswestry, the Rev. J. Matheson, B.A., minister of the Old Chapel, and others; and each scholar, after tea in the evening in the schoolroom, received a book in which was inscribed a record of the event of the day. The scholars of the National Schools dined in the pavilion on the Bowling Green, under the superintendence of Mr. T. L. Longueville, the Rev. Ll. Wynne Jones, curate of the Old Church, and other friends.

At Wrexham there was a general holiday on the wedding day, and tea was provided for rather more than 500 women. After tea the Bowling Green was opened for dancing. There was a public dinner, of course, and Lord Dungannon was the president, supported by Simon Yorke, Esq., Townshend Mainwaring, Esq., Rev. G. Cunliffe, vicar, T. T. Griffith, Esq., and other gentlemen. And on the day after the wedding there was a ball, under the patronage of Lady Cunliffe, Mrs. Fitzhugh, Mrs. Yorke, Mrs. Panton and other ladies.

The demonstrations at Welshpool were rendered more than usually interesting by the presence of Sir Watkin and his fair bride. The day chosen was the one on which the Montgomeryshire Yeomanry assembled for their eight days' exercise; and, the baronet being colonel of the regiment, that body formed a no inconsiderable element in the proceedings. Sir Watkin and Lady Williams Wynn were met at the Buttington Gate, on the Oswestry road, by the mayor and corporation; an address of congratulation was presented to them, and they were then escorted into the town. A public dinner was held in the Town Hall, under the presidency of J. D. Corrie, Esq., supported by John Williams, Esq., The Mayor, at which Sir Watkin was present. A sum of £150 had previously been collected, which was distributed in various ways to the poor and to the schools. And as part and parcel of the proceedings at Welshpool—although the act was highly interesting to the county generally—we must include the presentation of a set of new standards by Lady Williams Wynn to the Yeomanry Cavalry. This was done on the Review Day, and the colours being duly "consecrated" by the Ven. Archdeacon Clive, her ladyship, in presenting them, said:—

Major Lord Seaham, Officers, Non-commissioned Officers, and Privates of the Montgomeryshire Yeomanry Cavalry;—from childhood I have been taught to consider myself, heart and soul, a Welsh woman. It is, therefore, a source of deep gratification to me, that one of my first acts after coming to reside in the Principality, should afford me an opportunity of testifying, however inadequately, the interest and regard I must ever entertain for a regiment, raised by my uncle, and now commanded by my husband. Allow me, gentlemen, to present these standards to the regiment, with my warmest prayers for its continued prosperity, and for your own individual happiness. I do so in the full assurance that those to whom I now entrust them will maintain the high character for loyalty and discipline which has ever distinguished the regiment; and that they will transmit that character to their successors, bright and untarnished as they received it. For the warmth and kindness of your welcome, accept my grateful and heartfelt thanks. It proves that you do not consider me as a stranger; but that you are willing, for the sake of those who have gone before me, whose name I have always borne, and still continue to bear, to extend to me some portion of the affection which you have hitherto evinced for that name. God bless you all.

Lady William Wynn, as she delivered this little address, was supported by the Countess of Powis, Lady Williams, the Ladies Herbert, &c., and was surrounded by a brilliant staff. We need scarcely add that her ladyship's eloquence was not lost on her large audience.

Another interesting occurrence marking the wedding was the laying of the foundation stone of a new Corn Market and Reading Room at Wenlock, South Shropshire. Most of our readers probably know of the intimate connection of the family of Wynnstay with the borough of Wenlock, and Sir Watkin having generously granted a site for the new building, the inhabitants fixed on the wedding day for commencing proceedings, and the day was observed as a general holiday. Miss Wayne laid the foundation stone, and the Rev. W. H. Wayne, the vicar, Sir George Harnage, Bart., W. P. Brookes, Esq., W. Jeffreys, Esq., and other leading inhabitants of the district, took a prominent part in the proceedings.

The marriage rejoicings elsewhere we must dismiss with shorter records, or we shall never complete our book within the limits assigned to it. At Bala there was a dinner, with Sir R. Vaughan, Bart., and W. W. E. Wynne, Esq., as presidents; and distributions to the poor. At Llanidloes the dinner was presided over by Messrs. T. E. Marsh and T. Hayward; and there was a procession of children and a plentiful supply of good things for them. Ruthin was the scene of great rejoicing; liberal subscriptions were made for the poor; rural sports were provided for the people, and the grand banquet was under the presidency of John Heaton, Esq., of Plas Heaton, and J. E. Madocks, Esq., of Glanywern. At Llanfyllin more than £60 was collected to spend in celebrating the day, the chairmen of the proceedings being Mr. Martin Williams, of Brongwyn, and Mr. W. Humffreys, of Llwyn. Llangedwyn, as may be supposed, was hearty in its demonstrations, and Llanrhaiadr joined with it in making the day memorable. A little over £200 was subscribed, which was expended in the usual manner, and at the dinner which concluded the proceedings we find the names of R. M. Bonnor Maurice, Esq., J. Hamer, Esq., Rev. E. W. O. Bridgeman, Rev. R. Williams, Rhydycroesau, J. Perrott, Esq., J. Gill, Esq., W. Evans, Esq., Glascoed, J. J. Turner, Esq., and various other well-known inhabitants of the district. Rhuabon, in addition to its feastings, was gaily decorated, and the chief members of the committee included the Rev. R. M. Bonnor, Messrs. Richard Jones, Belan Place, G. H. Whalley, R. W. Raikes, E. Tench, G. Stanton, R. Wright, R. C. Roberts, E. L. Ward, Morris, draper, C. Wigan, Allen, &c. There was such a procession at the remote and beautifully situated village of Llanbrynmair as we may suppose to be unique in the history of Welsh villages, for it is said that more than two thousand people joined in it; and at Llanarmon there was a large distribution of beef to the poor, with sports for the youngsters, and a dinner for the well-to-do, at which the late Mr. Thomas Jones, of Brook Street, Oswestry, presided, supported by Mr. Lewis, of Plas-ty-Ceiriog.

The well-known local names of Whitfield, Hughes, Richards, &c., are, of course, associated with the rejoicings at Llansilin; and although that parish had contributed largely to the Llangedwyn subscription list, they had a gala day of their own, and a dinner, over which the Hon. W. Bagot, M.P., presided. At Meifod " the lads had their sports, the lasses their dance, but no boy could be found to climb the pole, so the new hat on the top of it was contended for in a donkey race." A procession marched through Llangollen, made up of School children, quarrymen, and tradespeople, numbering over a thousand; and there was a public dinner at which Mr. Godfrey, Mr. Charles Richards, Mr. A. Reid, and Mr. R. Edwards, were presidents. There was also a dinner at Ellesmere, the Rev. E. H. Dymock and Mr. Richard Wynn acting as presidents, supported by Messrs. W. Sparling, of Petton, T. S. Oswell, G. Salter, T. J. Rider, Sheraton, W. Hassell, &c.; and at various other places, including Newtown, Llanymynech, and The Lawnt, the wedding day was celebrated.

One permanent memento of the Marriage of Sir Watkin and Lady Williams Wynn is the clock on the front of the Wrexham Town Hall.

WYNNSTAY AFTER THE FIRE.

DESTRUCTION OF WYNNSTAY BY FIRE.

DURING the night of Friday, the 5th of March, 1858, the old mansion of Wynnstay was almost totally destroyed by fire, which was not discovered until nearly three o'clock on Saturday morning, and then the flames had made terrible progress. It was supposed that the fire originated in a room under the library, and the first alarm was given by one of the servants, who had not gone to bed until a late hour, and of course, supposed all to be safe then. At the time there were guests in the house, including the Earl and Countess Vane (now Marquess and Marchioness of Londonderry), and two children, the Honourable Wellington Cotton, (now Lord Combermere) and the Hon. Mrs. Cotton, Captain Bulkeley, and Mr. Hugh Williams. As quickly as possible Sir Watkin alarmed the household, and the scene presented was appalling. Some of the servants barely escaped with their lives, and Lord Vane had only time to rush to the rescue of his son, who a moment later would have been lost. The fire-engine on the premises was at once put into requisition, but without the smallest effect, and an effort was made to save the more valuable of the paintings. But so dense was the smoke that the attempt had to be abandoned, and several family pictures, amongst others, were destroyed. Most disastrously a south-west wind was blowing at the time. Soon it became evident that much valuable property must inevitably be lost, but amongst the salvage, was the celebrated picture of the Wynnstay Hunt, and a Dressing Case, set in gold, which had been presented to Lady Williams Wynn, on the occasion of her marriage, by the Montgomeryshire Yeomanry Regiment, of which Sir Watkin is the colonel. Up to four o'clock it was unknown in Ruabon that so sad a catastrophe was taking place at their very doors, but as soon as it was known the whole village turned out to lend a helping hand. At five o'clock the fire was at its height, the wind had increased to a hurricane, and the rain came down in torrents. To quote a report of the scene as related by an eye-witness, " At that hour the whole of the front of the hall was one fearful blaze, which raged with terrific violence, burning with a fury awfully majestic. Gold, silver, precious stones; statuary and ornamental work; costly furniture and drapery; books, MSS., and paintings, worth thousands of pounds—and some that money could not replace, were all merged in one fiery mass, that lit up the country for miles around." Jewels to the amount of £5,000, the property of Lady Vane—to the amount of £1,500 belonging to the Hon. Mrs. Cotton, were in the wreck; the magnificent library was entirely destroyed;—and here the loss was irreparable, for it contained the only copies of ancient Welsh MSS., and many rare works. The cellars were almost the only portion that did not suffer, and wines, valued at £40,000, were uninjured.

The services of an experienced member of the Fire Brigade from Watling Street were put into requisition after the fire, when the whole of the debris lying under certain rooms was carefully put through sieves under his superintendence. This patient and painstaking labour was rewarded by the discovery of several articles of jewellery belonging to Lady Vane, the Hon. Mrs. Cotton, and Lady Williams Wynn. The compiler of these pages was present when a barrow-full of ashes was discharged on the floor of a brew-house. To ordinary eyes it looked a very ordinary load of rubbish indeed, but the experienced eye of the professional soon detected a dirty little mite, which turned out to be a diamond of the first water, and worth £600.

An event like this, it may readily be imagined, was one that would call forth the deep and hearty sympathy of a large circle; and the newspapers of Wales and the Borders for weeks afterwards contained reports of "Meetings of Condolence." But first of all a public meeting was held at Wrexham on the Wednesday after the fire, for the purpose of considering what should be done, when the Vicar, the Rev. G. Cunliffe, suggested a "shilling subscription," for the "purpose of presenting a casket of jewels to Lady Williams Wynn, as an expression of esteem and good will." This was, of course, not to be merely a local affair, and a committee was appointed, with Mr. T. T. Griffith, treasurer, to solicit subscriptions from all quarters. On the following day Sir Watkin attended a meeting at Wrexham, for the purpose of receiving an address of condolence, which was presented to him by the late Mr. T. Edgworth, the first mayor of the new corporation. Sir Watkin, in reply, said—

It is true a man does not know his best friends until he is overtaken by sorrow. It is that which tests it. I and my family have lived many years, aye, generations, amongst you, and in such a calamity as has now occurred, it is a consolation to know that we are sympathised with—I will say that we are beloved by you. In these circumstances I know not whether I shall look up to the higher, or look down to the lower, of my neighbours, who, in my distress, urged me to use their homes as an asylum, or to the kind-hearted collier who came and worked up to his middle in water on that boisterous morning. I say I do not know whom to thank the most. All did their best, and I thank all from my heart. It is difficult to find words adequate to express my feelings to many I see around me. My wife, too, thanks you, and thanks her God that no casualty occurred—no life was lost during the calamity. * * * * I do hope that those who may live at Wynnstay in the future will see by these addresses that I have not lost the good opinion of my friends and neighbours.

In reply to the Rhuabon address, which was presented by the Vicar, the Rev. R. M. Bonnor (now Dean of St. Asaph), Sir Watkin expressed his hope that if God spared his and Lady Williams Wynn's lives, they would be of as great use as they could to those kind neighbours who had been of such use to them. A meeting was also held at Rhuabon to discuss the " shilling subscription " project, and a suggestion was made by Mr. Whalley that a painting of the old house of Wynnstay —as a companion picture to that of the Wynnstay Hunt,—should form the memorial, rather than a casket of jewels. Further discussion, in which the Rev. W. Venables Williams, the Rev. A. F. Taylor, Mr. Morris (post office), Mr. Tench, Mr. R. C. Roberts, and Mr. Martin took part, led to the determination of the meeting to confine the subscriptions from Rhuabon to the immediate district, and not to join in the county subscription set on foot at Wrexham, and the form the memorial was to take was left an open question.

The presentation of the Oswestry address took place on March 17, in the presence of a large assembly, including Mr. J. T. Jones (the mayor) and Mrs. Jones, Mr. and Mrs. Cartwright, Mr. J. and the Misses Croxon, Rev. Ll. W. Jones, Rev. G. Cuthbert, Mrs. and Miss Donne, Mr. and Mrs. Wynne Thomas, Mrs. T. Minshall, Dr. and Mrs. Harvey Williams, Mr. Sabine, Mr. J. Jones (solicitor), Mr. E. Williams, jun., Mr. Ward, The Donnett, Mrs. G. Owen and Miss Jones, Mr. E. Oswell, Mr. and Mrs. D. Lloyd, &c. Lady Williams Wynn was unavoidably absent. At Llangollen the presentation took place in the open air, no building in the town being sufficiently large for the throng. The Rev. W. Edwards, vicar, was deputed to act as spokesman, and an address, in Welsh, to the assembly, was given by the Rev. J. Pritchard, Baptist minister, after Sir Watkin had thanked his friends and neighbours for their mark of sympathy. A public meeting was held at Ruthin, the Mayor (J. Maurice, Esq.), presiding, at which an address of sympathy was read by the Rev. the Warden, and moved by Mr. Peers and Mr. Gabriel Roberts. It was also resolved to contribute to the shilling subscription fund. Meetings of condolence were also held at Welsh-pool, Llanbrynmair, Cefn Mawr, Machynlleth, Llangedwyn, Llan-gadvan, Llansilin, Llanrhaiadr, Llanarmon, Llanfair-caereinion, Rhos-llanerchrugog, Llanfyllin, Bala, Denbigh, Dylife, St. Asaph, Llan-uwchllyn, and other places, at all of which it was agreed to send addresses of sympathy to Sir Watkin and Lady Williams Wynn.

The Calvinistic Methodists, a religious body including nearly half the inhabitants of North Wales, at their "sassiwn" in April, 1858, held in Llanidloes, discussed the propriety of presenting an address to the baronet. The idea was, of course, received most cordially, and a deputation was appointed to make the presentation at Welshpool on the occasion of Sir Watkin's visit to that town at the annual meeting of the yeomanry. The deputation consisted of Richard Davies, Esq., (then High Sheriff, and now M.P. for Anglesey), John Foulkes, Esq., J.P., Aberdovey; Thomas Roberts, Esq., Mayor of Llanidloes; Rev. J. Hughes, of Liverpool; Rev. D. Morgan, of Welshpool; Mr. Ebenezer Cooper, of Llangollen; Mr. P. M. Evans, of Holywell; Mr. R. Hughes, of Wrexham, &c. The Rev. J. Hughes, in presenting the address, remarked that it came from a community possessing a thousand chapels, and comprising within its pale 70,000 members, and 125,000 Sunday scholars. It was their earnest hope that the lives of Sir Watkin and Lady Williams Wynn, so providentially saved, would long be preserved and greatly blessed. In thanking them for the address, Sir Watkin said :—

He had been waited on by a great number of deputations—both from bodies con-nected with the Established Church, and from those that were not—who had expressed their sympathy on account of the great calamity that had occurred to the House of Wynnstay. The kindness thus shown had been a source of much gratification to Lady Williams Wynn and himself. He regretted that there was not greater unanimity amongst Christians, inasmuch as all had the same object in view, namely, to publish and make known the saving truths of the Gospel. He believed that had it not been for the labours of the Dissenters in Wales, the great mass of the people would have been without religion. He felt himself honoured by the address they had just presented him with, and he hoped those sentiments of respect that had been expressed would never be forfeited by him, nor that he should prove undeserving of them.

At Wynnstay there are also preserved addresses from several of the Freemasons' Lodges on the occasion of the fire, and, in addition to that from the Presbyterians, there is one from the Protestant Dissenters of Penegoes and Darowen, and another from the Dissenters of Machynlleth.

PRESENTATIONS AFTER THE FIRE.

ON Wednesday, May 11, 1859, the *Oswestry Advertiser*, in giving
an account of the presentation of Memorials arising out of
the "Shilling Subscriptions," said, "We are glad to know that the
proposal to present Lady Williams Wynn with a 'casket of jewels'
has been abandoned, and are informed that a very general feeling is
entertained in favour of the erection of almshouses." It was then,
however, too late to act upon this general feeling, because £250 of the
amount collected was already presented in four different forms, and,
after stating this, the paper went on to say, "It is now too late to say
what might have been done, and all we have to do is to offer our
congratulations to Sir Watkin and Lady Williams Wynn on the proud
position they hold in the affections of their neighbours. The scene in
Wynnstay park on Monday was one never to be forgotten. Ten
thousand happy faces smiling a welcome, and ten thousand voices
uttering hearty cheers, are not every-day events, and the estimable
lord and lady of the estate must have felt that such sympathy as they
have received on their return to the Principality is some equivalent for
the loss of their mansion."

To explain this, we should say that after Wynnstay was
destroyed, Sir Watkin broke up his establishments in England and
Wales for a period, and went on the Continent. On his return to
Denbighshire he was waited on, and a day was fixed for the first of
the presentations in connection with the fire. The one to which we
allude was that of a Bible, accompanied by an illuminated address, the
gift of eight thousand subscribers in Rhuabon and district, and the
place chosen for the ceremony was under the magnificent old oak we
have previously referred to in these pages. The Rev. R. M. Bonnor,
the Vicar, and Mr. Morris (post-office), a leading Nonconformist, made
the presentation, and after Sir Watkin had given a suitable reply,
Lady Williams Wynn said :—

H

I cannot leave my husband the honour of thanking you for the very handsome gift which you have just presented to us. Believe me that it will ever be treasured as one of the most valued possessions of our new house. The deep and affectionate sympathy shown to us by all our neighbours has more than compensated for all the trials we underwent last year. I feel how unable I am to give expression to my feelings in words, but let me assure you that no gift could have been selected so consoling to our feelings as that sacred volume, and I will now only add my fervent supplications that the prayer with which you have accompanied this gift may be heard, and that it may indeed prove a blessing upon our home.

At the conclusion of her ladyship's speech, Mr. Roberts, surgeon, stepped forward, in the name of the tenantry of the Rhuabon district, to present Sir Watkin and Lady Williams Wynn with a timepiece, costing a hundred guineas; and an address. These being suitably acknowledged the vast assembly dispersed.

The testimonials of esteem from Rhuabon were followed up by others from Llangedwyn and Llanarmon. At noon, on May 10, 1859, a large number of tenants and friends assembled in front of Llangedwyn Hall, and everything being arranged, the Rev. Hugh Heaton, in the name of the inhabitants of Llangedwyn, presented Lady Williams Wynn with a splendid piece of workmanship, in the form of a casket, made of oak saved from the ruins of Wynnstay. On a gold plate affixed this was stated, and it was added that it was given "by her friends and neighbours at Llangedwyn, young and old, rich and poor, as a token of sympathy and affection." Lady Williams Wynn in the course of her reply said :—

To this place I have returned in every season of sorrow or of joy, sure that in either I should receive from you that sympathy which nothing but mutual and well-proved friendship can inspire. . . . . My heart is too full to permit me to say more than to assure you that I shall deeply value this casket as a memento both of old Wynnstay and of dear Llangedwyn, and as an additional bond of affection between us all.

The Rev. W. Jones then stepped forward, and, in the name of the parishioners of Llanarmon-dyffryn-Ceiriog, many of whom, he said, were tenants of Mr. West, presented Lady Williams Wynn with a splendidly-bound Duoglott Prayer-book—Welsh and English. After her ladyship had received the book, Sir Watkin replied in suitable terms, and with three cheers for the family the company separated.

The next presentation we have any record of is that of a sword to Sir Watkin from the Montgomeryshire Yeomanry, of which the baronet is the commander. This bears the following inscription :— " Presented to the Lieut.-Col. Sir Watkin Williams Wynn, Bart., by the officers, non-commissioned officers, and privates of the Montgomeryshire Yeomanry Cavalry, as a small token of their sympathy and regard upon the occasion of the disastrous fire which destroyed Wynnstay, 6th March, 1858."

The grand presentation—the result of the " shilling subscription "— came off on Saturday, December 15, 1860. Happily the idea of a casket of jewels had long before been abandoned, and a picture decided on. This picture was exhibited in May, 1860, at the Royal Academy, and was thus described in the official catalogue :—" Sir Watkin and Lady Williams Wynn : presented as a token of sympathy and affection by 11,947 Cymry to Marie Emily Williams Wynn, in remembrance of the merciful protection vouchsafed to her and Sir Watkin, on the 6th of March, 1858, when Wynnstay was destroyed by fire." The picture is by F. Grant, R.A., and when we first saw it in the Academy, although the portraits of Sir Watkin and Lady Williams Wynn were excellent, and a favourite horse and hound had been skilfully introduced by the artist, there was a somewhat bare look about the painting ; but when the picture was presented it had been wonderfully improved by the addition of appropriate scenery in the back-ground. The Rev. G. Cunliffe, the originator of the idea of a shilling sub- scription, was deputed to make the presentation, and the ceremony took place in the Town Hall, Wrexham.

Amongst those present on the occasion, in addition to Sir Watkin and Lady Williams Wynn, were Captain Charles Wynn, Mr. Grenville Wynn, Colonel Herbert Wynn, M.P., and Mrs. Herbert Wynn, Sir Hugh Williams, Captain and Mrs. Peel, the Ven. the Dean of St. Asaph and Mrs. Bonnor, Captain Bulkeley, Lady Marshall, Colonel Taylor, Mr. and Mrs. Wingfield, &c., &c.

In making the presentation, the Vicar of Wrexham gave an outline of the labours of the committee in the matter of the testimonial, and, pointing to the picture, remarked, " There behold the happy result of all our discussions and all our anxieties. If you consider that the artist has done justice—if you think the likeness of Lady Williams Wynn is happy and true—if you can trace there that benign expression which forms the chief feature in her countenance, then the committee will be highly gratified, and amply rewarded for their labours." The applause of the large crowd assembled to witness the ceremony amply proved that the labours of the committee were appreciated. Sir Watkin and Lady Williams Wynn both replied, and the company separated, a very large number adjourning to the Wynnstay Arms, where a public luncheon had been prepared, after which speeches were delivered by Mr. A. Howell, Mayor of Welshpool, Dean Bonnor, Canon Cunliffe, Mr. J. Clarke, Mayor of Wrexham, and others.

BIRTH OF A DAUGHTER.

THE friends of the House of Wynnstay, although they sincerely rejoiced in December, 1864, when a daughter was born, we need scarcely say did not herald the birth of the young lady with anything like the noisy acclamations that would have been called forth by the birth of an heir. "Louise Alexandra Williams Wynn," born December 21, 1864, was christened January 30, 1865; her godmothers were the Queen of Denmark and H. R. H. the Princess of Wales, and her godfather was Sir Hugh Williams, Bart. Congratulations poured in from all quarters, including, amongst others, the following addresses :— Llanvorda Tenantry; Boys of Rhuabon Grammar School; Boroughs of Ruthin, Denbigh and Welshpool; Tenantry and others of Llwydiarth ; Inhabitants of Rhuabon, Llanrhaiadr, Wrexham, Llangower, Llangollen, Oswestry, and Llansilin ; Tenantry of Llanwrin ; Manager and men of the New British Iron Co., Rhuabon, &c., &c.

Twelve months later Sir Watkin and Lady Williams Wynn celebrated the birthday of their little daughter by a grand ball, which also was intended to be a "housewarming ;" the new mansion being so far completed as to be eminently comfortable as a residence. On an earlier page we have referred to the new house as a "rather severe adaptation of the Louis Quatorze style." We believe the original design is by no means completed, and we question whether the house will ever assume the old-fashioned air of comfort and solidity of the mansion it has supplanted. The writer in the *Field*, already quoted, holds a different opinion, and believes "that 'Carthago Nova' will, in every way, far surpass the old building :" and he goes on thus to describe it :—"The new is in the Italian style, with beautifully laid-out parterres; internally the rooms are comfortable, and furnished in exquisite taste, a chimney piece in Lady Williams Wynn's room, carved in Rhuabon stone by a Welshman, being quite fit to compete with the efforts of foreign artists. The grand hall, too, is a very fine room, with splendid oak ceiling, copied, we think, from the Hotel de Ville at

MISS WILLIAMS WYNN.

MISS NESTA WILLIAMS WYNN.

Rouen." One striking feature in some of the rooms and passages at Wynnstay is the very large number of beautifully illuminated congratulatory and sympathetic addresses, presented to the family; we question whether all the mansions of Wales combined could produce such a collection. Many of these we have already enumerated, and we may here remark,.for the benefit of all future "Testimonial presenters," that in several cases the names of the chairmen signing the documents are lost to posterity, simply because the writers have made use of common ink which time has faded.

To return to the ball. It is described as one of the most brilliant scenes it is possible to imagine. A very distinguished company was entertained by Sir Watkin and Lady Williams Wynn for several days prior to the occasion, amongst whom were Lord and Lady Macclesfield, the Ladies Parker, Lady Theodora and Lord Richard Grosvenor, Lord Powis and Lady Harriet Herbert, Lord Combermere, Lord Methuen, Captain and Lady Frances Lloyd, Miss Kenyon, Lady Egerton of Tatton, Miss Egerton, Baron Beck Fries, Captain and Miss Bulkeley, Mr. B. Ferrey, Col. Wynne, Capt. Rowley, Mr. Needham, Mr. R. Cholmondeley, Mr. Methuen, Mr. W. R. M. Wynne, M.P., Mr. Owen S. Wynne, Mr. W. S. Williams, Captain Denman, Mr. LLoyd, Leaton-Knolls, the Hon. R. Hill, &c., &c.

The guests at the ball included representatives of all the leading families of North Wales and the Borders; the list extends to nearly a couple of columns in the newspapers, and dancing was kept up with spirit to the strains of the band of the Life Guards.

The birth of the daughter was commemorated by Owain Alaw and Talhaiarn, in music and song; the former skilfully arranging the old Welsh air "Meillionen," commonly known as "Sir Watkin's Delight," to words by the latter, a sample of which we give in the following :—

> O, dyma hardd fesen o hên dderwen gref,
> A fu'n oesi ganrifoedd drwy fendith y Nef;
> Ei gwraidd a ddwfn-dreiddiodd i galon y wlad,
> A'i theg frig sy'n wyrddlesni o fythol barhâd :
> I lenwi ei swydd safed Gwalia yn syth,
> A chyduned plant Awen yn lawen ddi lyth,
> Mewn hwre i Syr Watcyn,—Syr Watcyn am byth !

With the portrait of Miss Williams Wynn, we also give one of Miss Nesta Williams Wynn, the younger, and only other child of Sir Watkin and Lady Williams Wynn.

THE WYNNSTAY HUNT.

IN the year 1851 a " Hunt Picture," which has become celebrated
by the engraving of it so often seen, was presented to Sir Watkin
on a fine hunting morning, when the hounds met at Wynnstay. The
idea originated with the Hon. Major Cotton, now Lord Combermere,
and Mr. Brancker, of Erbistock Hall, and what were intended to be
likenesses of the following ladies and gentlemen are depicted in the
painting :—Sir Watkin Williams Wynn, Captain Lloyd, Thomas Lloyd
Fitzhugh, Esq., The Hon. Edward Kenyon, William Brancker, Esq.,
Roger Palmer, Esq., Colonel Boates, Earl Vane, Countess Vane,
Edmund Peel, Esq., Captain Bulkeley, Mrs. Clement Hill, The Hon.
Major Cotton, Master Myddelton Biddulph, John Hamer, Esq., Rowland
Hunt, Esq., William Sparling, Esq., Thomas Oswell, Esq., Mr. Walker,
(the Huntsman), The First Whip, the Rev. E. H. Dymock, Henry B.
Clive, Esq., The Second Whip, Thomas Hugh Sandford, Esq., Philip
William Godsal, Esq., Master Mainwaring, Mr. Henry Crane, Simpson,
(Head Groom), and Mr. Campbell. The late Col. Myddelton Biddulph
made the presentation speech, and there was a grand breakfast.

The taste for fox-hunting, says " Cecil," in the *Field* newspaper of
March, 1867, took its rise in the Wynnstay family at a very early
period ; as soon, indeed, as it became a sport patronized by the wealthy
and the great. " A very unhappy event occurred on the 26th of September, 1749, when the first Sir Watkin was killed by a fall from his
horse when hunting with his own hounds near Wrexham." The baronet
who met with the untimely death, our authority goes on to say, " had
hunted the country for many years, and at some period after the accident Mr. Leche, of Carden, succeeded to it." The same or another
" Cecil," writing in *Bell's Life*, three years earlier, referring to the
death of the first Sir Watkin, says : " I cannot obtain any authentic
information to connect that baronet as having a pack of his own, and
come to the conclusion, therefore, that he was hunting with Mr.
Leche's hounds when the unfortunate accident occurred." A writer in

Baily's Magazine, in 1863, assumes that the first Sir Watkin was a master of hounds, and says, in reference to the present baronet, " For a master of fox-hounds Sir Watkin may be said to possess hereditary qualifications, inasmuch as his great-grandfather was as celebrated for his attachment to the sport as for his Jacobite opinions, which occasionally exposed him to some personal inconvenience. In fact, in 1745 he was compelled to quit Wales, and partake of the hospitality of his friend, the Duke of Beaufort, at Badminton, and a picture is still in existence at Badminton, in which the Duke and the baronet are looking over a racehorse." Touching this picture, we may remark in passing that there was a duplicate at Wynnstay, which was burnt in the fire of 1858, and it has been replaced by the courtesy of the present owner of the original, who commissioned an artist to paint a copy for Sir Watkin.

From the authorities we have already quoted, and from various newspaper extracts, we glean the information we are about to give respecting " The Wynnstay Hunt." We are told that about the last year or so of the eighteenth century, Sir Richard Puleston occupied the country, and continued to do so, with an occasional interruption, till the time when he sold his hounds to Lord Radnor to hunt the Berkshire country, which was in 1834. When Sir Richard was otherwise engaged, the Cheshire, at the time Sir Harry Mainwaring was master, came occasionally. In 1834 the late Sir Watkin hunted one portion of it, and the Shropshire hounds the other. The late Sir Watkin, however, only kept a small pack of hounds, with which he hunted fox or hare, having but a limited scope for the enjoyment of his pastime. In 1837 Mr. Leche succeeded Sir Watkin, having hunted a part of his father's country with some that had been occupied by Mr. Richard Puleston ; and this continued until 1840. Mr. Leche then resigned, and the hounds and the country came into the possession of Mr. Artry, of Lightwood Hall, who disposed of the hounds together with the rights appertaining thereto, to the present Sir Watkin, in 1843. To these were added the pack kept by Mr. Grant, at Kilgraston, in Scotland (the brother of the artist who painted the portraits of Sir Watkin and Lady Williams Wynn after the fire), and subsequently some hounds were purchased from Mr. Musters, and other lots at Mr. Foljambe's sale in 1845.

The present Sir Watkin, as we have already stated, was born in 1820, and succeeded his father in 1840. " He was educated at Westminster, and after a course of study at a private tutor's, in Derbyshire, he entered at Christ Church, Oxford, in October, 1837. Here he remained for nearly two years ; but academical discipline interfering too much with his pursuit of the chase, and other congenial amusements, he took leave of the University and joined the 1st Life Guards, in July, 1839. Four years in the household troops was sufficient to gratify his military ardour, and he forsook London and London life to fulfil his duties as a landlord." We have seen that his great-grandfather was a sportsman, and in his day Welsh manners and customs were not quite in accordance with modern ideas. Even as lately as the time of Pennant, as we have stated in an earlier page of this work, substantial furniture was more in keeping with the ways of a gentleman's living than frippery ornaments; and this will be readily seen when we state that at Wynnstay, " which was always full of company, the gentlemen used to dine in one room and the ladies in another, the latter merely coming into the gentlemen's room to have their healths drunk, and saw no more of their husbands until they were carried either to their beds or their carriages."

The second Sir Watkin, although he kept hounds and maintained the hospitality of his race, was, as we have already seen, of a different turn of mind, and loved the society of musicians, actors, and artists, more than he did that of horses and hounds, and preferred the late hours of a London drawing-room in the season to hearing " bright Chanticleer proclaim the dawn," in Wales, on a fine hunting morning. With the third Sir Watkin, and father of the present baronet, the sporting feeling revived, when military ardour had been satisfied, and this Sir Watkin " originated the good old-fashioned system of keeping ' open house' at Wynnstay," which, however practicable then, could hardly be pursued in the present day. Our portrait of the late Sir Watkin represents him as the elders of the present generation remember him, crippled from the accident we have described in a previous page. For years before he died, we are told, " he was moved about in an arm-chair; and to enable him to enjoy his whist, a frame was constructed to hold his cards, which a person behind him used to play for him by his dictation." In earlier life he was esteemed an excellent shot and a good horseman, " and frequently have he and his brother Charles been known to swim across the river Dee, on the coldest winter day, after a wounded bird," for of course at that time retrievers were unknown.

The present Sir Watkin was only twenty-three years of age when he took upon himself the duties of master of the hounds. His first huntsman was Will Grise, who was first whip to the Shropshire under Will Staples. His career was short, for he died after enjoying the post for two or three seasons, and was succeeded by Jack Woodcock, first whip, who, however, only kept the position one year, when, the

Fifeshire being given up, the services of John Walker were secured,
" Merry John," as he was sometimes called from his cheery way with
his hounds.   In the spring of 1858, at the end of Mr. Walker's tenth
season, it was decided to present him with a testimonial from the gentlemen of the hunt, as a mark of their appreciation of his ability and " un-
tiring zeal to show sport," and the presentation was made on the opening day at the kennels, and took the form of a silver hunting horn, pair of
silver spurs, and a purse of four hundred guineas.   The present Lord
Combermere made the presentation, and about a couple of hundred
gentlemen took lunch in the open air on the occasion, although the date
was the first of November.   In 1866 Walker retired, and was succeeded
by Charles Payne, of the Pytchley, who still occupies the post.

One of the authorities we have quoted gives the following description of Sir Watkin's hunting country :—

Sir Watkin Wynn's country comprises a portion of Denbighshire, Shropshire, and
Cheshire, extending eastward to Market Drayton, where it joins the North Stafford-
shire.   The northern extremity reaches into the neighbourhood of Chester, and eastward of this division it meets the country hunted by the Cheshire hounds.   Shrewsbury
defines the southern boundary.   Two lines of railway may be described as traversing
pretty nearly the eastern and western margins.   The Great Western from Shrewsbury
to Wrexham, and on to Chester, being westward, and the London and North Western
eastward, and another line from Oswestry through Whitchurch, and on to Crewe,
passes nearly through the centre of the country ; thus steam conveyance is available
to all the places of meeting.   On the Great Western the stations are Shrewsbury and
Baschurch, both of which are in proximity to Fitzbridge; Baschurch to Little Ness, Pres-
ton, Boreatton, Ruyton, Petton and Middle; Rednal station to the Queen's Head, Pradoe,
Woodhouse, and Cockshutt ; Oswestry station to Halston, St. Andrew's, and Oteley
Park ; Gobowen station to Selattyn and St. Martins ; Chirk station to Chirk Castle
and The Quinta; Ruabon station to Bodylltyn, Newbridge, Overton, Bryn-y-pys, Dud-
dleston, Cockbank Gate, Penley Hall, Bangor, Worthenbury; Wrexham station to Cefn
Hall, Erddig, Marchwiel, Shocklach, Chorlton Hall, Malpas, Cuddington Heath, Sarn
Bridge, Pentre-Bychan ; Wrexham or Gresford stations to Gwersyllt Hall, Acton,
Aldersey Hall, Holt, and Carden Hall.   The stations on the London and North-
Western line commence with Yorton, available for Acton Reynold and Broughton
Hall ; Wem, station for Cockshutt, Loppington, Soulton Bridge, and Hawkestone;
Prees station, Sandford; Whitchurch station for Twemlows, Cloverley, Hanmer, Iscoyd,
Sharvington Park, Styche, Hinton House, and Maesfen.   Near the line from Oswestry
to Whitchurch, are at Ellesmere station, Oteley Park, The Pigeons, Pleasant Grove,
and Stockett Gate ; Bettisfield station, Gredington, Hanmer, Green Dragon, and
Bettisfield Park.

Space fails us to go into particulars about the dogs and the horses,
but " Cecil " gives so interesting an account of the kennels that we are
sure our readers will thank us for reproducing it :—

The admirable construction of the kennels demands a brief description of them.
A spacious boiling-house is supplied with two "coppers," as they are commonly,
though erroneously denominated, inasmuch as they are never now-a-days constructed

I

of that poison-generating metal, but usually of cast iron. These, however, are made of wrought iron, which is doubtless far superior, and eventually more economical, as masters of hounds will acknowledge who have experienced the frequent burstings of which the cast metal is susceptible. These wrought iron ones are made at a factory not far distant from Ruabon. The feeding-room adjoins the boiling-house, contiguous to which there is an ante-room, well adapted to pass a pleasant hour on "the flags," protected from the bleak blasts of a November morning. In this room there is a bath, through which the hounds are passed, having been fed, after hunting. They are then conducted into a spacious room, covered with straw, called a drying-room, where they are allowed twenty or thirty minutes to roll, revel, and lick themselves, before being shut up in their lodging room for the night. This is an excellent arrangement. There are altogether four commodious lodging-rooms, with yards, and three hospitals where invalids may repose, free from the intrusion of officious companions. Over the principal lodging rooms are the sleeping apartments for the men, and a passage runs the whole length, with trap-doors in the floor opening immediately above the hounds' benches, so that if any disturbance arises in the night the men have only to raise one of the trap-doors to quell the riot. The same contrivance also serves to pass clean straw through, which is stored in a loft at the end of the building. The meal, of which there is a capital store of very superior quality, is kept on the same landing, and there is an arrangement by which it is conveyed through the flooring with great facility into the boiling-house.

Since this was written the so-called " coppers " have been superseded by a large steaming apparatus, by Annies and Barford, of Peterborough.

The fine old hound, Royal, who is depicted in Grant's picture, deserves honourable mention here. He was in his prime fifteen years ago, and was then described as having " truly exquisite " neck, shoulders, legs and feet. He was a son of Lord Fitzwilliam's Singer and Sir Watkin's Rarity, a daughter of Lord Yarborough's Harper and Remnant. The " strain " from which Royal descended came from Mr. Foljambe's, at whose sale Sir Watkin is said to have given 390 guineas for five couples of hounds. The best dogs in Sir Watkin's pack are of the Royal breed.

Sir Watkin's weight renders it necessary that the horses he rides should be those of the very "highest pretensions," and Mr. Simpson, the stud-groom, whose likeness appears on the Hunt picture, sees after this department most satisfactorily. When Sir Watkin broke up his establishment in 1858, after the fire, his horses were sold by auction, and the prices they realized pretty well proved the quality of the stock. King Dan, a splendid horse, six years old, in his second season, was bought by Mr. Anderson for £460. Cromaboo realised £315, and was bought by Mr. Darby. Mr. Gillmore was the purchaser of Caster, at £283, &c., &c. The most attractive "lot," was Cassio, by Murphy, which was knocked down to Mr. Anderson at 620 guineas. As soon as he was put up he was started at 200 guineas, and Mr. Richard Tattersall, jun., who conducted the sale, had scarcely time to utter a word before the price ran up to 600 guineas. Up to this price the principal bidders were Mr. Anderson, of London, Mr. Percival, of Wandsworth, and Mr. Darby, of Rugby, well known dealers. When the horse was purchased, Mr. Anderson was well cheered by the company, and Captain Clement Hill complimented him on being the possessor of the best horse in England.

The sale, our readers may be sure, attracted a very large company. Amongst those present were the Marquis of Stafford, Lord Hill, Lord Macclesfield, Lord Wenlock, Lord Grosvenor, Sir Henry Edwardes, Sir Piers Mostyn, Sir J. R. Kynaston, Sir R. Brooke, Sir Humphrey de Trafford, Sir Vincent Corbet, Sir Charles Slingsby, Sir Thomas Boughey, Hon. H. Powys, Hon. L. Kenyon, Hon. Col. Cotton, Hon. Rowland Hill, Major Owen, Captain Lloyd, Mr. E. Wright, Mr. Roger Palmer, &c., &c. And before we pass on we may remark that when the late Sir Watkin, in 1814, went to France, prepared to fight his country's battles, Messrs. Tattersall sold five of his hunters, at their London establishment, for sixteen hundred and eighty guineas.

We need scarcely add that on his resumption of the duties of master, Sir Watkin became the possessor of a stud unsurpassed by any that had preceded it. The first in point of age and in merit is, unquestionably, Comet, a wonderful dark chestnut horse that has survived the eighteen seasons which have elapsed since the fire. *Baily's Magazine* in 1863 describes him as " the pick of the basket ; " " B." in the *Field*, December, 1865, says, " Comet is a dark chestnut, with a few grey hairs throughout ; his shoulders are magnificent, and his limbs masses of muscle ; if we could point out a defect it is perhaps a slight degree of lightness in the barrel ; but he is capital over the back and loins—we should say he is 16. 1, but he objected to the indignity of being gauged ; he is indeed a splendid animal, and his action throughout very grand." This writer had a pretty good opportunity of judging, for he " saw him going hock deep with Sir Watkin " on the day of his visit. " Cecil," who visited Wynnstay in the spring of 1867, corroborates all that has been said of this favourite horse, and says that then " Comet, a chestnut of vast bone and power, stood in very great repute."

Amongst Sir Watkin's horses there are also Locomotive (mentioned by one writer as early as 1865), Franciscan, Gilbert, Tigress, Doctor, Planet, and The Nailer : and those for Mr. Payne's riding include Quilp and Fenian (who received honourable mention in *Bell's Life* ten years ago), also Cuckoo, Margravine, Gentleman, and Albert. Of all sorts there are about 55 horses in Wynnstay stables.

SIR WATKIN'S ILLNESS AND RECOVERY.

EARLY in 1875 it became very generally known that Sir Watkin was seriously unwell, and it is no exaggeration to say that hundreds of warm-hearted Welshmen felt regret as keen as if the life of one of their own kith and kin had been in jeopardy. The malady was a dangerous one—carbuncle on the neck—and for some weeks the baronet suffered greatly, and, at one time, we believe, fears were entertained of his ultimate recovery. However, towards the end of April Dr. Fox and Mr. Spencer Wells reported their patient in a fair way speedily to be removed from London, and the newspapers gladdened many hearts by spreading the welcome intelligence. Soon after this Sir Watkin did, for a few days, return to Wynnstay, and whilst there performed an act unique, perhaps, in the history of baronets, and one that only a pure-minded and simple-hearted Christian gentleman could have performed. On Sunday, the ninth of May, in the accidental absence of the clergyman from Wynnstay chapel, " Sir Watkin proceeded to the desk, and read the whole service ; and the worthy baronet, it is said, regretted that want of notice prevented him from being prepared with a sermon." This was just such an act as Sir Watkin could do, and do gracefully, and it is worthy of remark that although the so-called " Religious Newspapers " of the day—usually far more bitterly opposed to each other's views than is ever found to be the case in Secular journals—all recorded the fact, not one could be found to cavil at the conduct of the baronet.

About the middle of May, 1875, Sir Watkin left Wynnstay for the Continent, under the advice of his medical men, where he remained for some weeks, and when it was known that he had returned to Wales—convalescent—at once addresses of sympathy and congratulation poured in from various quarters.

Sir Watkin and Lady Williams Wynn arrived at Wynnstay on the 3rd of July, and they found Rhuabon quite prepared to receive

GLANLLYN, BALA LAKE.

them with every mark of hearty congratulation. The village itself was gaily decorated, and the servants at Wynnstay, under the guiding hand of Mr. Middleton, the head gardener, had, as if by an enchanter's wand, changed the unattractive entrance into the park into an archway of flowers. A halt was made at this arch for the purpose of presenting an address, signed on behalf of the tenants, by R. C. Roberts, H. C. Murless, David Jones, Samuel Lewis, and Robert Lloyd. Dr. Roberts having made the presentation, Sir Watkin in reply said :—

I did not expect this act of kindness, and have not prepared any reply to your kind address, but I am very much obliged to you; Dr. Roberts, for all the kind things you have said, and must thank you all most heartily for your kindness. I am very glad to come down again amongst my friends, friends from whom I have always received unvarying kindness. Many of you I have known from childhood. My journey to France has done me good, but I am very happy at being home once more.

Before the party (which now included Miss Williams Wynn and Miss Nesta Williams Wynn) proceeded on their way, Mr. Owen Hughes, in the name of " those residing within the park " presented an address congratulating the baronet on his recovery. This was signed as follows :—Owen Hughes, Henry Simpson, John Evans, Wm. Leighton. J. S. Laycock, P. Middleton, E. Rowlands, Henry Lewis, W. Brewer, A. H. Franke, S. Micklewright; W. Cartwright, M. Bayley, P. Edwards, Hugh Ll. Roberts, Catherine Cocks, Elizabeth Harding, Margt. Richardson, J. Barfoot, T. Endersby, M. Evans, &c., &c. At the top of the avenue another halt was made, to receive an address from the teachers and pupils of Miss Williams Wynn's school. The girls were drawn up in line, all wearing the scarlet cloaks and black hats Lady Williams Wynn had presented them with some months before ; and the address was read by Mr. J. S. Crofton.

On the 13th of July, Sir Watkin visited Llanbrynmair, where he met with a most enthusiastic reception. He arrived from Towyn by an evening train, accompanied by Lady Williams Wynn and Mr. Owen S. Wynne, and was met at the station by the Rev. J. W. Kirkham, the Rector, the Rev. R. Trevor Owen, and other well-wishers. A large procession, made up of tenantry and villagers, was formed, and an address was presented, signed on behalf of a committee, by O. Thomas, chairman, E. Vaughan, treasurer, and T. Vaughan, secretary. A second address, on behalf of the school children, was presented by Mr. Evan Davies.

The Llanuwchllyn address was presented at Sir Watkin's Merionethshire residence, Glanllyn, on the borders of Bala Lake. The Rev.

J. S. Jones, the Vicar, headed the deputation, and the address was also signed by Edward Edwards and Evan Davies. At the same time the Rev. W. Roberts presented an address on behalf of the parishioners of Llangower, concluding his speech with the following " Englyn " :—

> Coed llwyddiant a ffyniant heb flaelu,—I
> Syr Watkyn a'i deulu ;
> A'u cysur fo yn cynyddu,
> O oes i oes medd fy yspryd i.

Of course at Llangedwyn the reception of the popular baronet after his recovery from illness was very hearty. This took place on the 27th of August. Sir Watkin and Lady Williams Wynn were met in the village by a troop of the Montgomeryshire Yeomanry, under the command of Captain Gill, accompanied by the band ; and the school children from Llanrhaiadr, Llansilin, Llangedwyn, Trefonen, Llanarmon, and Llanvorda, mustered in large numbers. The Rev. R. Trevor Owen presented an address, from the district generally, and one from Llanfihangel was presented by the Rev. Edward Evans, which was signed by him as rector, and by the Rev. E. V. Owen, of Llwydiarth, Rev. R. Jones, Dolanog, and about forty-five tenants and others. Mr. Owen, of Newtown, as soon as the addresses were presented, photographed the party on the terrace, which included Sir Watkin and Lady Williams Wynn, the Misses Williams Wynn, Miss Cocks, Mr. Charles Williams Wynn, M.P., and the Misses Williams Wynn, Coedymaen, Mr. and Miss Dugdale, Llwyn, Mr. and Miss Hamer, Glanyrafon, Mr. and Mrs. Owen Wynne, Miss Essex Cholmondeley, the Misses Owen, Colonel Bonnor and Miss Berthon, Captain and Mrs. W. Gill, Mr. George Williams, the Rev. W. Williams, Llanrhaiadr, Rev. E. Evans, Llanfihangel, Rev. E. Owen, Llwydiarth, Rev. Mr. Morgan, Llanrhaiadr, Rev. D. P. Evans, Trefonen, &c., &c. The children, 700 in number, afterwards had tea, their wants being supplied by Miss Williams Wynn, Miss Mary Nesta Williams Wynn, Miss Cocks, the Misses Owen, Mrs. T. Longueville, Llanvorda, Miss Jones and Miss West, Llansilin Vicarage, Miss Berthon, Miss Whitfield, Glascoed, Mrs. Richards, Tanygraig, Mrs. Foulkes, Llwynymaen, Mrs. D. J. Hughes, Mrs. Sides, Mrs. Moreton, Abercynlleth, Mrs. Daniel, Mrs. D. Foulkes, Mrs. Thomas, Mrs. Peate, Mrs. Owen, Banhadle, Mrs. Hughes, Cefnhir, Mrs. Buckley, Mrs. A. Evans, Mrs. Hughes, Pentreshanel, Mrs. Stokes, Miss Roberts, Miss Jones, Trefonen Hall &c., &c.

We must curtail our record of other addresses. The Corporation of Wrexham presented one on August 21st ; and on the 24th of the same month there was a grand Volunteer Inspection in Wynnstay

Park, of the corps of which Sir Watkin is Lieut.-Col. The officers present were Lieut.-Col. Sir W. W. Wynn, Major West, Captain Conran, Adjutant, Captain Yorke, Junior Adjutant, Captains Adams, Lloyd, Williams, Tottenham, and T. Bury; Lieutenants Pugh, Evans, Morris, Crawford, T. Williams, Aspinall, Price, Barratt, Tanqueray, Hughes, Parry, J. Parry Jones, Humphreys, Roberts, and Ellis. At the conclusion of the drill, Colonel Cooper addressed the corps in complimentary terms, after which the men were marched to two large tents, which had done duty the previous day at a flower show. Here Major West presented Sir Watkin with a congratulatory address, magnificently illuminated, and placed in a massive gilt frame. The remaining addresses, to which we have referred, included the following :—Parish of Llangurig (signed by Rev. J. Evans, vicar, J. Hamer, T. Lewis, J. Watkin, and H. L. Davies), Congregational Church of Llanbrynmair, British School of Llanbrynmair, &c., &c.

In acknowledgment of all these addresses Sir Watkin, a few months later, sent out invitations, on a large scale, to his principal tenantry, inviting them to a

GRAND BANQUET AT WYNNSTAY,

the following report of which, with the list of guests, we take from a newspaper of November, 1875 :

Seldom probably since there were Wynns at Wynnstay has the family seat of the greatest of Welsh families seen a more magnificent banquet than that which, on Friday, October 29th, the baronet, in acknowledgment of the addresses presented to him on his recent restoration to health, gave to his tenantry in a pavilion pitched under the walls of his mansion. Invitations had been sent out east, west, north, and south, to all tenants down to a rental of £10, and about seven hundred responded to the call of their landlord, and bid him good bye before he goes for his Mediterranean cruise. The day was fine— that is, although it was dull, gloomy, and cold, there was, for a wonder, no rain, and at the end. of an October such as we have had, one is grateful for small mercies.

What with ordinary and what with special trains, most of the guests reached Rhuabon by little after mid-day, and at twelve the noble army of farmers might have been seen streaming thick and fast up the wide avenue, the autumn breeze showering down on their sober raiment the yellow leaves from the stalwart beeches and chesnuts, whose beautiful but dreary autumn dress was vanishing into the mournful nakedness of winter. Montgomeryshire, Merionethshire, Denbighshire, and the Shropshire border tenants all marched along together, and perhaps a very practised and acute eye could have told the county, and possibly, by their accent, the district of many, but to the general glance there seemed little to distinguish these Welsh farmers from their English brethren, and what little there was, was only the common darkness of complexion transmitted from the Britons, which has, from the time of Hengist, distinguished the aborigines from the " blue-eyed heathen," and the comparative absence of the fifteen and eighteen stone men whom Shropshire and Norfolk seem to grow, but whom neither Wales nor America can fatten. The some five hundred Montgomeryshire men who attended came by special train, drawn by the engine " Sir Watkin," the carriages running through to Rhuabon. The unimposing Renaissance architecture of Wynnstay, with its low roofs and heavy dome-like projections, so very modern contrasted with the embattled walls and flanking towers of Chirk, and the—from a distance—more-feudal-than-the-middle-ages fortress of Brynkinallt, lent no aid to anyone imaginative enough to hark back the two hundred years which would transmute the black-coated and very prosaic railway travellers who trudged up the park, into troopers in jack boots and morions, or steel-clad men-at-arms and bowmen. The hounds with the scarlet-coated huntsmen and whippers-in, were out in front, and the stables and mansion were flung open for all, so there was plenty to do, and amusing it was to see the awe with which the folk from the hills stole on tiptoe along the corridors and through the halls, so sacred to them as the actual home and abode of the great Sir Watkin. From the organ gallery all sorts and conditions of music could be heard, Sir Watkin's organist, Mr. Sparrow, playing on the organ alternately with Mr. Lloyd Roberts on the harp, and " Ah che la morte " taking its turn with " The rising of the lark."

Hard by the pavilion the brazen clangour of the trumpets and drums of the Montgomeryshire Yeomanry Cavalry Band re-echoed down the park, and far away to cottages where " Kunstler Leben " is unknown, and farmhouses whose daughters had till then been ignorant of " Madame Angot's " ravishing airs. The interesting thing about the house, to those that had done it before, was the chapel, which has been restored. In the chancel were some fine carved oak seats adorned with grotesque heads, and a fine crimson and gold altar cloth, which with a lot of theatrical dresses, was actually thrown out of the window, at the time of the fire, and has lately been applied to its original use.

WYNNSTAY.

To the good old tune of the " Roast Beef of Old England " the crowd thronged into the pavilion, and soon the host and hostess appeared.

That the pavilion, marquee, or tent, however it may be termed, was of unusually ample proportions, will be inferred from the fact that over seven hundred people sat down to the dinner. It was a grand sight. Within its canvas walls were twenty tables placed across the tent, not lengthwise as is most commonly done, and at the side was a raised platform or dais, with table, on which the host and his personal friends were seated. The tables were covered with silver plate and vases of exotic flowers at intervals among the venison, beef, game, and pastry; ropes of evergreens festooned the airy roof, and the light supporting poles were wreathed alternately in holly, with clusters of red berries, and other evergreens—the work of Mr. Middleton, the gardener; while from the dais raised above the surrounding tables, where " aloft in awful state" Sir Watkin and his kinsmen and personal friends sat, sparkled and blazed a dazzling array of plate. Towering above the others by its size was the great and massive silver vase, inscribed in four languages, English and Latin, Welsh and Greek, " To Colonel Sir Watkin Williams Wynn, Baronet, the patriot leader of his brave countrymen during the Rebellion in Ireland and Invasion of France, as a memorial of his repeated voluntary services, the county of Denbigh presents this tribute of esteem and gratitude. MDCCCXV." On either side of this memorial of '98 were grouped gold cups, lettered " Chester Races, 1817," " Shrewsbury Races, 1818," and " Chester Races, 1818," and " Worcester," reminiscences of victories on the Roodee and elsewhere, whose heroes have long slept under the turf they once so proudly trod. There was a splendid silver salver engraved with the motto of the Wynns, " Nec me meminisse pigebit." Another gold cup, over a hundred years old, bore the inscription—" At the second annual meeting, won by Sir Watkin Wynn, Brown George. By the President, 1769." Behind these were, in frames, the addresses of the Llanvorda, Llangedwyn, Llanrhaiadr, Llansilin, Llanbrynmair, and other tenants, congratulating Sir Watkin on his recovery, with one from the " St. Oswald Lodge " of Freemasons.

Mr. C. H. Browning, of Paddington, was the caterer of the dinner, which was á la Russe. Its merits, as seven hundred Welshmen have gone forth to spread them over hill and dale, need not be enumerated here.

NAMES AND ADDRESSES OF THE GUESTS.

BANGOR PARISH.

Mrs. Margaret Ellis, Crab Tree Green
Mr. John Green, Crymbal Farm
,, William Jones, Penybryn Farm

CEMMAES PARISH.

Mr. David Jones, Craigfawr
,, Thomas Breeze, Ffriddfawr
,, David Davies, Groesheol
Mrs. Joanna Davies, Glan'rafon
,, Mary Jones, Rallt
Mr. John Davies, Tanyglannau

CARNO PARISH.

Mr. Owen Burton, Blaenglanhanog
,, John Richards, Caeauduon
,, John Morgan, Ffosddu
,, John Jones, Galltyfrondy
,, William Jones, Galltyfrondy
,, Thomas Breeze, Glanhanog Ucha
,, John Francis, Pickins
,, Joseph Jones, Tyddyn-tuhwnt-i'r pwll

DAROWEN PARISH.

Mr. Morris Jones, Castell
,, Hugh Hughes, Gwernbere
,, Edward Davies, Tynynant
,, Richard Davies, Tynynant
,, Humphrey Humphreys, Tyddyn Cogwalcog

ERBISTOCK PARISH.

Mr. John Weaver, Top Farm
,, Samuel Lewis, Park Eyton
,, Robert Morris, Caegwydd Farm
,, Thomas Morris, Caegwydd Farm
,, Robert Jones, Cefnydd Farm
,, Ambrose Withers, Rutters Farm
,, William Leighton, gamekeeper
Mrs. Eliza Daniels, Cross Foxes
Mr. John Thomas, Nanterral
,, Richard Taylor, Park Eyton
,, Joseph Thomas Boote, Lower Park Eyton
,, John Roberts, Fields Farm
,, William Brancker, Erbistock Hall

GARTHBEIBIO PARISH.

Mr. Evan Hughes, Cae'rlloi

Mr. Richard Hughes, Dolymaen
,, Gwen Jones, Nantydugoed

LLANGEDWYN PARISH.

Mr. Edward Davies, Cilmawr
,, Peter Williams, Cilmawr
,, Hugh Hughes, Penybryn
,, David Jones Hughes, Penybryn
,, Hugh Hughes, The Mill
,, Thomas Jones, Wernole Farm
,, Thomas Morris, Gellyfelin Farm
Rev. R. T. Owen, Plas Uchaf
Mr. Cadwaladr Ellis, The Gate Public House
,, Richard Thomas, Highland
,, Thomas Jones, Hendre Farm
,, Charles Vaughan, Wernypennant
,, William Sands, sen., Wernypennant
,, William Sands, jun., Wernypennant
,, David Foulkes, Tytanydderwen
,, Thomas Davies, Ddol Ucha
,, John Daniels, Tanllwyn

LLANRHAIADR PARISH, DENBIGH.

Mr. Thomas Hughes, sen., Gartheryr
,, Thomas Hughes, jun., Gartheryr
,, Robert Richards, Tanygraig Farm
Mrs. Mary Vaughan, Brynyhriw
Mr. Charles Davies, Banhadla Isa
,, Humphrey Hughes, Cefnhirfawr
Mrs. Alice Morgan, Rhydgaled
Mr. Thomas Evans, Tynyfedwen
,, Maurice Jones, Tytanyffordd
,, Allen Evans, Tynynant
Mrs. Mary Ellis, Henblas
Mr. Maurice Owen, Belaneinion
Mrs. Mary Kynaston, Fron Goch
Mr. John Davies, Pentrevelin
,, Richard Buckley, Frondeg Farm
,, Charles Buckley, Frondeg Farm
,, David Jones, Representatives of Tanygraig
,, David Edmunds, Cefn Farm
,, Robert Vaughan, Cryniarth
,, Robert Evans, Glantanat
Mrs. Ann Evans, Tynypistill
Mr. Robert Daniels, Caerfach Farm
,, John Edwards, Caerfach Farm
,, Edward Jones, Tybrith Farm

Mr. Thomas Williams. Efel Rhyd Mill
  „ David Evans, Trewern Isaf
  „ John Humphrey Evans, Wynnstay Arms
  „ Edward Buckley, Glaniwrch Uchaf
  „ Evan, Jones, Penrallt
  „ Evan Hughes
  „ John Vaughan
  „ J. G. Edwards

LLANRHAIADR PARISH, MONTGOMERY.

Mr. Charles Charles, Clynog Farm
  „ Edward Thomas, Caenant
  „ Charles Bibby, Frongoch
  „ Edward Pierce, Frongoch
  „ Charles Pierce, Frongoch
  „ Thomas Rees, Tanygraig Farm
  „ Evan Rowlands, Tanygraig Farm
  „ Evan Lloyd, Pentre Abermarchnant
  „ Evan Roberts, Tycerrig

LLANARMON-DYFFRYN-CEIRIOG PARISH.

Mr. John Jones, Gyrchynan Isa
  „ Thomas Jones, Gyrchynan Ucha
  „ Edward Jones, Gyrchynan Ucha
  „ Henry Evans, Glasaber
  „ John Jones, Cwm-y-Geifr

LLANSILIN PARISH.

Mr. Richard Richards, Glascoed
  „ David Richards, Glascoed
Rev. Walter Jones
Mr. Thomas Morton, Cross Foxes
  „ Bell Edward Richards,
  „ John Lloyd, Fron
  „ David Lloyd, Fron
  „ David Evan Jones, Penlan
  „ Griffith Morris, Pentregwynbach
  „ Edward Hughes, Representatives of, Derwendeg
  „ Edward Jones, Penygraig Ucha
  „ David Edwards, Golfa Isa
  „ John Hughes, Penygraig Isa
  „ Thomas Peate, Maestanyglwyden
  „ Thomas Edwards, Pwllymeirch
  „ Robert Sides, Golfa
  „ Thomas Ellis, Mount Sychart
  „ Charles Williams, Pandy Sychart
  „ Henry Williams, Pandy Sychart
  „ Edward Vaughan, Golfa Isaf
  „ John Wilson, Tygwyn

Mr. Morris Evans, Graigwen
  „ Richard Lloyd, Rhiwlas
  „ Richard Lewis, Nantrhiwlas Ucha
  „ J. Jones, Blaenrhiwlas Ucha
  „ E. Edwards, Blaenrhiwlas Ucha
  „ Evan Jones, Plastregeiriog
  „ John Jones, Plastregeiriog
  „ Humphrey Morris
  „ David Ellis. Hendu
  „ C. Charles, Hendu
  „ Richard Hughes, Tynycelyn Farm
  „ Thomas Morris
  „ John Hughes, Penrallt
  „ John Roberts, Penrallt
  „ Edward Davies, Graigwenfach

LLANFAWR PARISH.

Mr. John Jones, Brynmelyn
  „ Edward Williams, Gelligron
  „ James Parry, Bryndu
  „ Robert Evans, Hafod Tydyr
  „ William Jones, Tyddyntyfod
  „ John Williams, Tynant
  „ William Roberts, Tyddyn Scubor
  „ Humphrey Williams, Tynypistill
Mrs. Ellen Jones, Tyddynfrydlin
Mr. William Jones, Ysbyddadog
  „ Simon Jones, Nantyrhenglawdd

LLANYCIL PARISH.

Mr. David Edwards, Bryndu
  „ John Evans, Brynmoelucha
  „ Owen Owens, Cerrigllwydion
  „ David Owens, Cerrigllwydion
  „ John Jones, Frondro
  „ John Williams, Gwernhefin
  „ T. Ll. Anwyl, Bala
  „ Evan Owen, Waen Bryncoch
  „ John Roberts, Waen Bryncoch

LLANUWCHLLYN PARISH.

Mr. Richard Williams, Alltygwine
  „ Robert Jones, Bryniau
  „ John Jones, Braichceunant
  „ Hugh Roberts, Bryngwyn
  „ David Davies, Brynllech
  „ Robert Parry, Brynllech
  „ John Jones, Buarthmeini
  „ David Pugh, Blaenlliw Isaf
  „ Joseph Williams, Blaenlliw Uchaf
  „ Robert Williams, Blaenlliw Uchaf

Mr. Hugh Jones, Bryncaled
 „ David Jones, Blaencwm
 „ Cadwaladr Jones, Bryn
 „ David Jones, Caergai
 „ William Jones, Coedtalog
 „ Henry Jones, Cefnprys
 „ John Evans, Castell
 „ Henry Parry, Tynybwlch
 „ Robert Parry, Tynybwlch
 „ Cadwaladr Jones, Cefnperfedd
 „ Thomas Jones, Cefnperfedd
 „ Edward Howells, Graigytan
 „ Robert Evans, Cwmtylo
 „ Owen Edwards, Caerhys
 „ Edward Edwards, Penygeulan
 „ Thomas Jones, Cefngwyn
 „ Owen Evans, Cwmonen
 „ John Evans, Cwmffynon
 „ Thomas Williams, Cae Llwyd
 „ Edward Rowlands, Dwrnudon
 „ Evan Edwards, Drwsynant
 „ John Cadwaladr Williams, Drwscae-
     gwenyn
 „ Rowland Williams, Drwscaegwenyn
 „ Robert Roberts, Dolhendre Ucha
 „ Thomas Jones, Deildre, Tygwyn
 „ Evan Jones, Dolfudr
 „ Ellis Rowlands, Tynyfron
Mrs. Jane Davies, Dolbach
Mr. William Thomas, Eagles Inn
 „ Morris Jones, Eithinfynydd
 „ William Hughes, Goat Inn
 „ Henry Jones, Gwerngrug
 „ Henry Holt, Glan'rafon
 „ David Parry, Graig
 „ David Williams, Tyddyn'ronen
 „ Thomas Rowland, Hafodyrhaidd
 „ Henry Davies Parry, Hafodyrwyn
 „ Griffith Jones, Hendre
 „ George Rowlands, Hendre Mawr
 „ John Jones, Lone
 „ Edward Watkins, Lone
 „ David Jones, Lone
 „ William Jones, Lone
 „ David Roberts, Llettycrippil
Mrs. Margaret Davies, Llwynpiod
Mr. John Rowlands, Llys
 „ Robert Jones, Llwyngwern
 „ Howell Jones, Llwyngwern
 „ Robert Jones, Llwyn Llwydyn
 „ John Jones, Maesgwyn

Mr. John Evans, Nantydeilie
 „ John Jones, New Inn
 „ John Jones, Nanthir
Mrs. Ellen Lloyd, Pentre
Mr. John Thomas, Plasmadoc
 „ Lewis Jones, Pantgwyn
 „ John Jones, Pantclyd
 „ Evan Davies, Prys
 „ David Roberts, Pursau
Mrs. Margaret Jones, Pantyceubren
Mr. John Rowlands, Pandymawr
 „ Edward Morris, Pantsaer
 „ David Jones, Rhydybod
 „ Thomas Williams, Rhydsarn
 „ Wm. Pierce, Ronwydd
 „ Griffith Roberts, Talybont
 „ Edward Roberts
 „ John Edwards, Tyddyntelin
 „ Henry Parry, Tyddynllywarch
 „ Robert Roberts
 „ Thomas Roberts, Trawscoed
 „ Edward Edwards, Tynybryn
 „ Evan Evans, Tycoch
 „ Thomas Davies, Tymawr
 „ Rowland Jones, Tymawr
 „ William Robert Jones, Tynycornel
Mrs. Elizabeth Jones, Tynrhos
Mr. Thomas Edwards, Tydu
 „ Thomas Jones, Tanybwlch
 „ Hugh Edwards, Tynyfedw
 „ John Jones, Wern
 „ John Rowlands, Werglodd Ddu
Rev. J. S. Jones, Werglodd wen
Mr. Robert Williams, Wernddu
 „ John Pugh
 „ Rowland Rowlands, Rhydydrain
 „ Robert Morris, Tynycae
 „ Thomas Thomas, Nantllyn
 „ Robert Roberts, Tymawr

LLANFYLLIN PARISH.

Mr. Thomas Jones, Blaenycwm
 „ Thomas Williams, Cammen
 „ Edward Watkin, Cammen
 „ Thomas Jones, Cammen
 „ W. Davies, Gwaelod, Cammen
 „ Thomas Evans, Groes
 „ Edward Jones, Hendre
 „ Evan Thomas, Llawrycwm
 „ David Lloyd, Lloran
 „ John Smith, Pentrepoeth

Mr. Robert Roberts, Rhosfawr
„ Thomas Davies, Tynymynydd,
„ William Davies, Tynymynydd
„ David Evans, Tynycoed
„ Griffith Jones, Tanyfoel
„ Robert Jones, Tanyfoel
„ Robert Thomas, Wynnstay Arms

LLANWDDYN PARISH.
Mr. John Lloyd, Abermarchnant
, Griffith Evans, Brynfedwen
„ William Williams, Glanrhyd
Mrs. Elizabeth Owen, Nanteinion
Mr. Thomas Jones, Nantlacher
„ Humphrey Lloyd, Gwreiddie

LLANFIHANGEL PARISH.
Mr. Robert Evans, Brwynog
„ David Evans, jun., Brynglas
„ Rowland Evans, Bryn
„ William Williams, Bryn
„ Watkin Lloyd, Bryn Mawr
„ Rees Davies, Braichywaen
„ William Jones, Bryngogledd
„ William Williams, Cefncleisiog
„ Richard Owen, Cadwnfa Mills
„ Richard Parry, Cefn Halfen
„ Griffith Jones, Coedleos
„ William Jones, sen., Cuddig
„ John Jones, Ceunant
„ David Thomas, Moelerfyl
„ William Watkin, Moelerfyl
„ Thomas Jones, Cefn-y-coed
„ Rees Davies, Dolwar Hall
„ Evan Jones, Dolanog Mill
„ Richard Davies, Dolwarfach
„ Thomas Jones, Eithin Geifr
„ David Lloyd Barnett, Efel Llwydiarth
„ Thomas Parry, Farchwel Uchaf
„ David Thomas, Farchwel Ganol
„ John Jones, Farchwel Isaf
Mrs. Ann Humphreys, Fachwen Ganol
Mr. William Jones, sen., Fachwen
„ William Jones, jun., Fachwen
„ Thomas Jones, Fronlas
„ David Evans, Glanrhyd
„ Sylvanus Edwards, Llwydiarth Hall
„ Robert Roberts, Llwynhir
„ David Roberts, Llwynhir
„ Henry Davies, Llettypiod
„ William Davies, Llwynymoelae

Mr. William Davies, Llettyllwyd
„ Benjamin Davies, Lletty'r Deryn
„ Thomas Jones, Lletty'r Meirch
Rev. Edward Evans
Mr. Thomas Owen, Llettyshenkyn
„ David Edwards, Llettypiod
„ William Gittins, Moelfronllwyd
„ Nathaniel Owen, Moelddiwid
„ Jacob Owen, Melinwnfa
„ John Jones, Mynydd-dwlan Isaf
„ Edward Jones, Mynydd-dwlan Uchaf
„ Lloyd Jones, Melindwr
„ John Ellis, Mynyddhir
„ Thomas Rees, Melinygraig
„ Joseph Gough, Pen'rarddlas Fach
„ David Lloyd, Pen'rarddlas Fawr
„ Evan Evans, Pendugwm
„ Evan Jones, Penisaf-y-llan
„ Evan Williams, Public House
„ John Price, Pentreheryn
„ David Jones, Pandy Llwydiarth
„ Evan Humphreys, Pontllogel
Rev. Edward V. Owen, Pontllogel Parsonage
Mrs. Elizabeth Evans, Penyrallt
Mr. Evan Williams, Pantglas
„ Thomas Jones, Penybryn
„ Thomas Ellis, Rhiwlas
„ David Watkin, Rhydlleche
„ David Jones, Tymawr
„ William Williams, Tygwyn
„ Pryce Morris, Tycoch
„ Edward Rogers, Tynewydd
„ David Davies, Tanygraig
„ Edward Edwards, Tymawr
„ David Davies, Tynycul
„ Ellis Jones, Tanllan
„ David Evans, Tynyshettin
„ William Jones. Tynycelyn Mawr
Mrs. Elizabeth Parry, Tynymaes
Mr. Robert Thomas, Tyarygraig
Mrs. Jane Lewis, Tynyrhos
Mr. David Owen, Ty Isaf o'r Glyn
„ Edward Edwards, woodman

LLANGADFAN PARISH.
Mr. Humphrey Ellis, Blaendyfnant
„ Evan Evans, Representative of, Caer Mynech
„ Henry Thomas, Cyffin
„ Lewis Hughes, Dyfnant

Mr. Evan Thomas, Dol Howell
  „ Edward Mills, Hafod
  „ Joseph Jones, Pantrhydynog
Mrs. Miriam Davies, Tynyfedw
Mr. Richard Jones, Tyntwll

LLANFAIR PARISH.

Mr. Maurice Davies, Goat Inn

LLANERFYL PARISH.

Mr. John Matthews, Abercannon .
  „ Evan Davies, Brynmawr
Mrs. Mary Williams, Cringoed Cottage
Mr. Cadwaladr Thomas, Cannon Farm
  „ John Roberts, Cwmderwen
  „ Thomas Jones, Reps. of, Dolfrwynog
  „ Isaac Jones, Dolwen Uchaf
  „ Robert Thomas, Dolygarregwen
  „ Hugh Thomas, Dolygarregwen
  „ Rees Jones, Doleceinion
  „ Richard Roberts, Dolydd
  „ Evan Roberts, Dolydd
  „ Edward Vaughan, Hafodybeudy
  „ William Jones, Moelddolwen
  „ Thomas Davies Jones, Moelddolwen
  „ Morris Jones, Neinthirion
  „ Thomas Vaughan, Sychtyn
  „ Edward Hughes, Nantyreira
  „ Cadwaladr Thomas, Nantyreira

LLANGOLLEN PARISH.

Mr. Richard Davies, Plas Eglwyseg Farm
  „ Simon Hughes, Eglwyseg Mill
  „ Samuel Pugh, Eagles Inn
  „ William Jones, Hendre Farm
  „ Elias Jones, Tynyfron Farm
  „ Edward Davies, Dergoed Farm
  „ David Jones, Rock House Farm
  „ Robert Roberts, Tanybwlch Farm
  „ John Williams, Pentredwr Farm
Rev. E. R. James

LLANARMON-IN-YALE PARISH.

Mr. Price Jones, Miners' Arms

LLANFAIR-DYFFRYN-CLWYD PARISH.

Mr. William Eyton Lloyd, Graig Farm
  „ Hugh Jones, Garthgynan Farm
  „ John Denman, Glanrafon
  „ Thomas Roberts, Pentrecoch
  „ Samuel Owen, Tyntwll

LLANBEDR PARISH.

Mrs. Mary Evans, Caerfameth

LLANGOWER PARISH.

Mr. Griffith Evans, Brynbedwog
  „ William Jones, Brynbedwog
  „ Rowland Morris, Brynhynod
  „ John Jones, Cornelau
  „ John Roberts, Cwmhyfed
Mrs. Catherine Rowlands, Caeglas
Mr. John Morris, Ffynongower
  „ Edward Jones, Gyrn
Mrs. Blanche Rowlands, Llechwedd du
Mr. Morris Peters, Myrddin Marred
Mrs. Jane Humphreys, Maes Meillion
Mr. Zaccaria Jones, Pantymarch
  „ Owen Pugh, Pentrecogwrn
  „ Hugh Pugh, Pentrecogwrn
  „ William Jones, Tycerrig
  „ William Jones, Tyntwll
  „ Rowland Williams, Ty'n Rhos
  „ Robert Richards, Werddonbach
  „ Edward Jones, Wenallt
  „ Rowland Davies, Gilrhos
Mrs. Jane Roberts, Bryncocyn
Mr. Cadwaladr Jones, Ty Isa
Rev. W. Roberts, Erwlas

LLANWRIN PARISH.

Mr. William Williams, Brynmelyn
  „ John Jones, Bryngronwy
  „ Evan Evans, Cefngader
  „ Elias Rowlands, Cockshed
  „ Evan Jones, Cae Iago
  „ Einion Thomas. Cilgwyn
  „ Richard Edwards, Ceniwsbach
  „ Stephen Breeze, Esgirwion
  „ Lewis Evans, Esgirfor
  „ William Jones, Gelly
  „ Edward Hughes, Goed-ddol
  „ Henry Thomas, Gwernstableu
  „ Morgan Morgan, Melingaerig
  „ William Owen, Mathafarn
  „ Hugh Edwards, Maesycru
  „ Hugh Evans, Rhydygwiel
  „ Richard Ryder, Tyucha
Rev. Daniel Evans, Llanwrin
Mr. David Jones, woodman

LLANBRYNMAIR PARISH.

Mr. Evan Evans, Blaenycwm
  „ William Richards, Borthlwyd
  „ Thomas Jones, Brynaere
  „ William Pughe, Brynllys

Mr. Richard Jervis
„ Edward Edwards, Bryncoch
„ Thomas Jones, Braichodnant
„ Edward Owen, Belan
„ David Roberts, Brynbach
„ Thomas Richards, Clegyrnant
„ John Jones, Caeaugleision
„ Abiah Jones, Cwmffynon
„ Evan Jones, Clegyrddwr
„ Edward Morgan, Wynnstay Arms
„ David Evans, Cringoed
Mrs. Ann Roberts, Coed Prefyde
Mr. John Hughes, Cwmcainedd Uchaf
„ D. Evans, Coedglyniau
„ Thomas Watkin, Cefn
„ Edward Hughes, Caetwppa
„ Thomas Hughes, Caetwppa
„ David Evans, Clawddycoed
„ John Evans, Cwmcalch Ucha
„ Edward Jones, Cwmcalch Isaf
„ Edward Jones, Caelan
„ Evan Ellis
„ Edward Evans, Dolfawr
„ John Bebb, Dolfawr
„ Edward Jones, Dollyden
Mrs. Elizabeth Evans, Diosg
Mr. Richard Lewis, Ffriddfawr
Mrs. Elinor Evans, Foelfach
Mr. Richard Wigley, Fron
„ Hugh Francis, Fronlwyd
„ John Jones, Gerddigleision
„ Evan Jones, Gerddigleision
„ Richard Thomas, Gelli
„ Evan Morris, Hafod-y-foel
„ Andrew Roberts, Hafodwen
„ Richard Wigley, Hirnant
„ David Roberts, Lluastyfedw
„ Peter Jones, Llwyncelyn
„ Edward Evans, Llawrycoed
„ William Anwyl, Mwyers
„ Edward Breese, Maesgwion
„ Richard Jervis, Maesymdrisiol
„ Thomas Morgan, Nantycarfan
„ Daniel Jarman, Pwllmelyn
„ Richard Owen, Penybont
„ Edward Hughes, Pentrelludw
„ Evan Morgan, Pantglas
„ John Jones, Penybwlch
„ Hugh Hughes, Pentremawr
„ Vaughan Hughes, Pentremawr
„ John Jones, Pentremawr

Mr. Joseph Jervis, Rhydymeirch
„ Edward Peters. Rhiwsaeson
„ Edward Powell Parry, Rhiwsaeson
Mrs. Ann Owen, Tafolwern Mill
Mr. Samuel Breese, Tycanol
„ Evan Evans, Ty Uchaf
„ David Jervis, Ty Pella
„ Maurice Jones, Tynycoed
„ Morris Jervis, Tymawr yn Llan
„ John Davies, Tymawr
„ Richard Davies, Tynygors
„ John Hughes, Tynyrwttra
„ Evan Bebb, Talerddig
„ Evan Roberts, Tygwyn
Rev. J. W. Kirkham, Llanbrynmair
Mr. Richard Evans, jun., Ystradfach
„ Evan Jones, Ystradfawr
„ Richard Lewis, Eskairykelynen
„ Harry Smith, Tymawr

LLANIDLOES PARISH.

Mr. Richard Thomas, jun., Penclun

LLANGERRIG PARISH.

Mr. Thomas Lewis, Hirgoed
„ Maurice Jones, Hore
„ David Jones, Maesnant
„ Thomas Jones, Maesnant
„ Lewis Evans, Cilgwrgan

MARCHWIEL PARISH.

Mr. Joseph Forrester, Five Fords Farm
„ George Forrester, Five Fords Farm
„ W. Cheatham, Reps. of, Gwrychteg

MACHYNLLETH PARISH.

Mr. David Lewis, Cleirie
Mrs. Mary Jones, Boot Inn
Mr. Richard Evans, Cwmbyr
„ David Davies
„ John Breese
„ John Edwards
„ Richard Lloyd, Pandy, Dolgae
„ James Jenkins Reps. of
„ David R. Pugh, Dolgae
„ Griffith W. Griffith
„ William Griffiths, Reps. of
„ John Evans, Dolsaeson
„ Richard Jones
Mrs. Elizabeth Jones
Mr. Edward Morgan

Mr. Evan Jones
  ,, Rowland Wood
  ,, John Jenkins, Hengwm
  ,, Hugh Lewis
  ,, Edward Parry
  ,, John Henry
  ,, Henry Williams, Melin Dolgae
  ,, Owen Williams, Melin Dolgae
  ,, John Williams, Red Lion Inn
  ,, Evan Jenkins, Talbontdrain
  ,, Griffith Williams

OVERTON PARISH.

Mr. Edward Lea, Lightwood Hall Farm

OSWESTRY PARISH.

Mr. J. B. Murless, Wynnstay Arms
  ,, John G. Foulkes, Llwynymaen
  ,, Edward Whitfield, Trefarclawdd
Mrs. Margaret Davies, Mynydd Myfyr
Mr. Price Owen Williams, Fron Farm
  ,, Wm. Hughes, Pentreshannel Farm
  ,, John Morris, Oswestry
  ,, Thomas Stokes, Ty Tanymynydd
  ,, Joseph Evans, Plasdympling
Rev. D. P. Evans
Mr. Charles Dolby, Plasdympling
  ,, Thomas Mansell, Croesybach
  ,, Edward Price
  ,, Thomas Green, Llwynymaen
  ,, John Thomas, Pantyffynon
  ,, Richard Edwards, Penybryn
Mrs. Jane Jones
Mr. Thomas Evans, Nantygollen Farm
  ,, John Edwards, Pentregaer
  ,, Hugh Lloyd, Coedygaer
  ,, John Edwards
Mrs. Margaret Morris
Mr. Thomas Thomas, Cynynion
  ,, Allen Edwards, Cynynion
  ,, Thomas Edwards, Cynynion
Rev. Robert Williams
Mr. Stephen Jones, Brongoll Farm
  ,, Robert Evans, Representatives of, Rhydycrosau
  ., Robert Roberts
Mrs. Elizabeth Hughes, Cae Canol
Mr. Thomas Roberts, Llanforda
  ,, Thomas Longueville, Llanforda
  ,, David Davies, Bwlch Farm
  ,, Edward Roberts

Mr. John Thomas, Pandy
  ,, John Jones, Llanforda Uchaf
  ,, Owen G. Jones, Llanforda Isa
  ,, Richard Myles
  ,, David Davies
  ,, Thomas Morris, Pistill
  ,, Elias Davies
  ,, Charles Edwards
  ,, Thomas Morris
  ,, Jonathan Price
  ,, Hugh Davies

PENNANT PARISH.

Mr. David Davies, Cedig

PENEGOES PARISH.

Mr. John Rees, Abercarrog
  ,, Hugh Swancott, Bryntydor
  ,, Evan Jones, Begeilyn
  ,, Thomas Jones, Begeilyn
  ,, Griffith Jones, Begeilyn
Mrs. Ann Rees, Cefnyfrifol
Mr. Morris Evans, Camderyffordd
  ,, Rowland Roberts, Dyffryn dulas
  ,, Ralph Dean, Dylife, Llanbrynmair
  ,, John Evans, Melindeflasse
  ,, David Morgan, Melin Newydd
  ,, Thomas Evans, Mynachty
  ,, Edward Pugh, Nantyfydda
  ,, Owen Owens, Pandy Penegoes
  ,, Hugh Tudor, Rhosygarreg
  ,, John Hughes, Rhiwgam
  ,, Evan Williams, Rhoswidol
Rev. W. Jenkins, Dylife

RUABON PARISH.

Mrs. Mary Jane Roberts. Cinders Farm
Mr. Peter Wright, Plas Isaf Farm
  ,. Thomas Hughes
  ,. Thomas Wright, Church-street
  ,. J. S. Laycock, Hafod Cottage
  ,, John Lloyd, Dinhinlle Farm
  ,, John Green, Street Isaf
  ,, William Richards
  ,, H. C. Murless, Wynnstay Arms
  ,, Samuel Sparrow, organist
  ,, J. E. Yates, G. W. Railway Station
  ,, Edwin Wall, bookstall
  ,, William Lloyd, platform inspector
  ,, Edward Hughes, Church-street
  ,, William Morris, Church-street
  ,, John Rowland Jones, Church-street

Mr. John Parry, late Goat Public-house
„ John Smith, grocer
„ John Roberts, Park-street
„ Charles W. Wright, Rhos Farm
„ Thomas Griffiths, Ruabon Mill
Mrs. Maria Davies, High-street
Mr. Samuel Randles, Newbridge
„ Fredk. T. Morrish, Railway Terrace
„ David Jones, Cross Foxes
„ John Griffiths, Moreton Farm
„ Lewis Jones, Lower Moreton Farm
„ Richard Price, Cefn Farm
„ Edward Jones, surveyor Rhosymedre
Mrs. Rose Beckett, the Dee Tavern
Mr. Henry Dennis, Hafodybwch
„ Edward Morris, Church-street
„ William H. Hughes, Plaskynaston
   Foundry
„ William Davies, Cefn
„ Robert Griffiths, Cefn Bychan
„ Thomas Pemberton, Pontadam
„ John Tomley, Pontadam
„ David Roberts, Pontadam
Dr. Roberts
Mr. Robert Pemberton, Great Western
   Inn
Dr. Jones
Mr. John Davies, Ruabon
„ Joseph Hughes, Ruabon
„ H. R. Bowers, Chester
„ G. H. Whalley, M.P., Plasmadoc
„ Owen Hughes, Bodylltyn
„ Charles Payne, The Kennels
„ Henry Simpson, Wynnstay
„ John Evans, Machine Farm
„ Peter Middleton, The Gardens
„ Wm. Pemberton
„ George Thomson, New British Iron
   Company
„ John Garside, Plankynaston Coal
   Company
Rev. E. W. Edwards, Vicarage, Ruabon

RUTHIN PARISH.

Mr. Thomas Jenkins, Plasyward
„ Hugh Edwards, hatter
„ Robert Edwards, solicitor
„ William Jones Roberts, currier
„ William Lloyd, Wynnstay Arms
„ William Lloyd, solicitor
„ Edward Davies, glazier

TREFEGLWYS PARISH.

Mr. John Thomas, Aberbiga
„ William Edwards, Aberbacho
„ John Wigley, Dolgwyddol
„ Evan Owen, Llwynog
„ John Edwards, Nantyrhafod
„ George Hughes, Rhiwdefeidy

TRAWSFYNYDD PARISH,

Mr. John Jones, Bryncelynog
„ J. D. Jarrett, Blaencwm, Prysor
„ W. Pugh, Caegwair
„ Edward Thomas, Caerhonydd
„ John Roberts, Dolymoch
„ Edward Rowlands, Defeidiog Ganol
„ Morris Evans, Defeidiog Isaf
„ Hugh Roberts, Darngae
„ William Williams, Dolymynech
„ Thomas Davies, Dolhardd
„ John Davies, Fadfilltir
„ Pierce Edwards, Glanllynie duon
„ John Pugh, Gilfachwen
„ Rowland Williams, Gors
„ Robert Roberts, Havodygarreg
„ Griffith Williams, Llech Idris
„ Hugh Pugh, Rhiwgoch
„ David Roberts, Tanrallt
„ William Owen, Tyddyn Mawr
„ Howell Roberts, Twrmaen

WREXHAM PARISH.

Mr. J. B. Murless, Wynnstay Arms
„ Robert Harrison, Plascoch Farm
„ Thos. Acton, Rhydbroughton Farm
„ Thomas Hanmer, Turf Tavern
„ Francis Goodwin, Hop Pole Inn
„ W. J. Sisson
„ Edward Lovatt, Old Swan
„ Edward Lewis, Llwynknottia Farm
„ Edward Bevan, Sutton Green Farm
Mrs. Emma Johnson, Escles Farm

GRESFORD PARISH.

Mr. Edward Jones, Gwersyllt Mill
„ Job Lea, Gwersyllt Hall Farm
„ William Barrett, Gwersyllt
„ Robert Dodd, Gwersyllt
„ Thos. Anthony Harrison, Gwersyllt
„ David Roberts, Gwersyllt
„ John Allmand

K

At the time of the banquet Sir Watkin and Lady Williams Wynn were entertaining at Wynnstay, Lady Williams, of Bodelwyddan (sister of Sir Watkin), Captain Williams, Mr. C. Williams, Captain Bulkeley, Mr. W. W. E. Wynne, Captain Rowley Conwy, Lord Parker, Hon. E. and Miss Kenyon, the Rev. Studholme Wilson, and Mr. W. Jones, London (Gwrgant).

On the right hand of Sir Watkin, the host, was Lady Williams Wynn, with her little daughters, Miss Williams Wynn and Miss Mary Nesta Williams Wynn, and on his left Lady Williams, and besides the company just mentioned who were present, there were at the upper table—The Rev. Canon Williams, Rhydycroesau, Rev. E. Evans, Llanfihangel, Rev. R. T. Owen, Llangedwyn, Mr., Mrs. and Miss Yorke, Mr. and Mrs. O. S. Wynne, Mr. C. W. Williams Wynn, M.P., The Rev. Watkin Williams, Mr. Owen Williams, Mr. G. H. Whalley, M.P., Mr. and Miss Brancker, The Rev. A. L. Taylor, Miss Cocks, Mr. Denman, Chief Constable of Denbighshire, Mr. Longueville, Llanforda, Mr. O. G. Jones, Llanforda isa, &c.

Dinner being ended the Rev. Canon WILLIAMS (Rhydycroesau, Oswestry) returned thanks.

Sir WATKIN then called out amid great cheering—I am now going to drink to your very good healths and so will Lady Williams Wynn. "Iechyd da i chwi."

The loving cup then went round.

Sir WATKIN—Instead of saying ladies and gentlemen I will merely address you as my friends. With very few exceptions you are, I believe, Welshmen, and you will hear most of the toasts given you in your native tongue. Well, we are all loyal subjects of her Majesty, and while we are assembled together in this Principality ought to follow the habits of all loyal men and drink to our good sovereign's health. I give you the health of her Most Gracious Majesty the Queen.

Owain Alaw, "God save the Queen."

Sir WATKIN—Now, then, my friends, the next toast I have to offer to you is that of our Prince and Princess. We are sorry that his health has caused him to go abroad, but again, on the other hand, you must consider that on the countries which his mother reigns over the sun never sets. Since I have had the honour of being one of the representatives of this county in Parliament the Queen has annexed the government of India to her crown, and we must all acknowledge how wise it is in the Prince to go and see the wonderful Eastern countries of her realm. Perhaps it may be out of place for me to mention it, but when I consider that my maternal grandfather was one of those who worked largely in the annexation of the Indian Empire, it may be that those of my Montgomeryshire tenants who have been brought up on my estates, and know the cordial feeling which the representatives of that house and I have always had towards each other, are delighted as I have been that the Prince has gone to see that vast empire. As to the Princess I might to-day have shown you her picture when she was in her earliest years. I will not say she is an old friend of mine, but still my father and hers were on the most intimate terms, and therefore I trust they may induced to spend some time amongst you here. I have no right to say so, but I trust it. Therefore I cannot do better than give the health of the Prince and Princess of Wales.

Mynyddog, " God bless the Prince of Wales."

Sir WATKIN—I believe we are all of a peaceful nature, though many of you belong to the auxiliary forces. However, when I have got here the majors of two yeomanry regiments and also of the volunteers of the county I don't think I can do better than propose their health. When I look round I see many collected together who would be glad to defend your homes if unfortunately anything like it was necessary. But I am happy to be able to say that we may run back from year to year for 120 years since blood has been spilt by civil war in this country, and to find a foreign foe who has ever been on this ground one must go back to something like a thousand years. As representative of the forces I couple with the toast the name of Mr. Charles Watkin Williams Wynn, major of the Montgomeryshire Yeomanry.

Mr. C. W. W. WYNN—Friends and fellow countrymen,—I can honestly say that when some three weeks ago, at a dinner in my own county, I found myself senior representative of the land forces—army, militia, and volunteers—in the room, I was very much surprised, but how much more so must I be in the much larger assemblage I have now the honour of addressing. Little as I feel able to respond for the army I am quite sure no one who listens but knows it has on countless battlefields done its duty well and nobly, whenever called, and we may have thorough confidence it will do this again. I feel the more delicacy in responding, that a brother officer is here who holds the same rank as I do in the Yeomanry of this county, and on that ground Major Rowley Conwy should have been called on to respond and not myself. I am rather shocked to see he hides himself and has not come to the front on this occasion. It is a bad omen for the country when its officers hang back. But I must give him credit for the fact that however inclined to turn his back here he would not do so were he in front of his regiment. For the Yeomanry I can speak with special confidence. I have, alas, been now for some thirty odd years in the Yeomanry, and am quite certain that if that force was required it would do its duty well and efficiently at whatever sacrifice to the convenience or comfort of those belonging to it. The Yeomanry are an old force, and a most valuable one, and one our rulers would really be sorry to see extinguished. Perhaps it would be hardly too much to say it was the parent of the Volunteer service. The old Volunteers perished, and the only ones that remain are the Yeomanry, and it was much through our presence that the Volunteers nearly sixteen years ago sprang up like the armed men from the teeth of the dragon.

Sir WATKIN—The next toast I have to give you, after you have drunk the health of those who I hope will never be called on to defend us, is the health of those who minister to us. I know, looking on this large assembly, that we are not united in our manners of worship. I know that, though I have been brought up in our respected National Church, many of you here are not its members. Still I know that the ministers of other denominations have worked hard in distant parts among the hills to promote Christianity, and to them we all must give our thanks. Many of you come from the diocese of Bangor, where you have an excellent bishop, who, though a Scotchman, has learnt the Welsh language. In this diocese we have a bishop, one of the most eloquent on the bench, and one of the best Welsh preachers I know. Although I did not approve of all Her Majesty's late Government did, I think we may thank them for the bishop they have sent to us. I therefore give you the health of the Bishop and Clergy of the Diocese, and Ministers of all Denominations. May I couple with the toast the name of an old friend—Canon Williams—who has educated many of the present company, among them my respected friend, Mr. Owen Wynne, an example of the maxim "Spare the rod and spoil the child."

Canon WILLIAMS—I think I am the oldest clergyman here present, and it therefore falls to my share to return thanks for the health of the excellent Bishop, Clergy, and Ministers of all denominations. I wish I could make a speech worthy of the occasion, but I am sorry to say that is a gift I do not possess. The clergy of the diocese are under very great obligations to the noble family at Wynnstay, and among them stands out prominently one case where the glebe acres, the site for the school-room and the playground, are all the gift of Sir Watkin. He has always been a most liberal contributor to all church calls, and I therefore wish him a long life and every happiness. Hir oes i Sir Watkin.

Sir WATKIN—I give now the health of the Members of Parliament. We happen to have two present, and this is one of the few occasions on which they may be seen sitting side by side, for instead of doing that in the House, they have for a long time had the pleasure of admiring each other's faces. I give you the Members of Parliament, coupled with the names of Mr. Wynn and Mr. Whalley.

Mr. C. W. W. WYNN, M.P.—As Sir Watkin has very truly said, more than a dozen years or so Mr. Whalley and I have had the pleasure of viewing each other's countenances, but, notwithstanding this, we have as often as we have met, walked together in all that concerns the welfare or prosperity of the Principality. It is now more years than I care to remember since I last saw a gathering of this size at Wynnstay. Our host had just then attained his majority. Probably there are not a couple of dozen that now hear me that remember that day, but such is our hereditary attachment to the Principality, of tenants to landlords and landlords to tenants, that I have no doubt that of those who were then assembled, a very large proportion of the sons are listening to me to-day. It is a happy and a pleasant feeling, and one which I think the warmest antagonists of what has been called the feudal system would have some difficulty in finding fault with. The arrangement is voluntary and free. The tenants know what they have to expect, they know that those who have done their duty by the landlord and his forefathers are not likely to have to leave. I can fancy no prouder position than Sir Watkin occupies to-day. The warm, unsought-for congratulations of you, and not only of you here present, but of hundreds—I might almost say of thousands not here to-day—must have made an impression on a heart of stone. I doubt, indeed, whether there be any man now living short of him whose health we drank immediately after that of her Majesty—I mean the Prince of Wales—whose convalescence has excited so much satisfaction, or met with the same warm congratulations. It is a proud feeling that must extend not only to his own immediate family, but to friends more distantly connected. I can only say for myself it gives me not only a feeling of pride in my family, but in those who have so appreciated our common ancestors. I shall leave my friend, Mr. Whalley, to answer for himself, and so far as I am concerned I shall only thank you who are my constituents and who are not.

Mr. WHALLEY, M.P.—To what has been so admirably spoken by Major Wynn, I say that the House of Commons in my estimation is but a thing of yesterday in comparison with that which you constitute here to-day, with that which you represent —the sinew, the heart, and the soul of this country. Nor is the House of Commons anything more contrasted with the relations between landlord and tenant to which

Major Wynn has referred, and which are a good sign for the times we have to look forward to. The House of Commons may disappear to-morrow without a regret left behind, provided such relations should continue, such relations as subsist between Sir Watkin and his tenants. I and a few are here from Ruabon, and I take the liberty, on the part of my neighbours here, to welcome you, Sir Watkin, and to invite your friends from every part of the Principality to join in hearty congratulation that we see Sir Watkin so well that he can reciprocate our feelings, and to ask all to join in the earnest prayer and hope that the immediate motive of this gathering, that of bidding him adieu for a time, in order that his health may be completely re-established, may be attended with the best results. What I have to say in conclusion is this—and I say it with the utmost sincerity—to those who know him here and those who will be able to know him. Those who know him will think I speak what is very much the truth, so far as it is felt by those who have the best chance of knowing, by close neighbourship with Sir Watkin. I say there is not a spectacle in the whole world, not throughout the vast empire of Great Britain to which Sir Watkin has referred, and on which the sun never sets, which is more glorious and admirable than such a man as Sir Watkin, with the position in which he is placed and the influence he commands, doing his duty to his neighbours and to his tenantry, and to all who have relations with him. It is not merely in the manner in which he sustains his position; it is in the example he sets to all of us to do our duty in our position as he in his, and then there will not be a community in the entire empire of Britain of which her Majesty's Government can be more proud than of the community of Wales, which Sir Watkin stands at the head of. Allow me again to express the extreme gratification I have in meeting you all here, and to piously trust that Sir Watkin's absence may realize the desires and hopes of his friends, and that he may come back in the renewed firm health of the old days, to take again the high responsibilities that devolve upon him.

Owain Alaw, " Land of my fathers."

Mr. JENKINS said—I have the pleasure to propose a toast, and do so with great pleasure, inasmuch as there is not in North and South Wales a toast hailed from lord to peasant with greater delight than that of Sir Watkin and Lady Williams Wynn's health. Brother tenants, I ask you if we ought not to be proud, if we ought not to congratulate ourselves on our homes and families, and how shall we do it better than dining at Wynnstay with our landlord, drinking to Sir Watkin's perfect restoration to health. What, brother tenants, has been Sir Watkin's object in bringing us here to-day? It has, of course, been to recognize the desire of his tenantry to please him, and to bring us one nearer to the other by giving us to understand our homes are our castles, and by wishing us "God speed." Then I hope, gentlemen, that we are worthy tenants of a worthy landlord. I hope that as an encouragement we shall conduct our farms in the proper way, and it is the duty of every tenant to make what improvements he can. But I will now propose Sir Watkin's better health, and hope he may live for very many years to be of use to his country as he has been good to us, his tenantry, and that he may live long to be a joy and happiness to Lady Wynn and her daughters.

Owain Alaw then sang a partly Welsh, partly English, song on Sir Watkin, the refrain being

" There's none that loves the Cymry
Like Sir Watkin Williams Wynn."

Sir WATKIN, who was received with a tremendous burst of cheering, said—My friends, it has pleased God to allow me to recover from my severe illness this spring, and having since then received the kindest testimonials and visits from very many of my kind tenantry, it was the wish of Lady Williams Wynn and myself that I might assemble you here together to thank you personally with one breath. It is, as my cousin has said, many years since all my tenantry were assembled together here. It was before some of those here were born or thought of. Thirty-four years is a long while to have been spared to have had the pleasure and happiness of having such a tenantry as I have. As to the duties of landlord or tenants I have heard long discussions in another place, but I am happy to say that I don't think that during these many years we have had many difficulties. Excuse me if I tell you a story. Perhaps you may say it is bad taste in me, but I certainly did not quote it in the House of Commons. It was a curious fact that when people were throwing out that no man would invest money without leases in any profession except farming, I could in the next breath have remarked that Cobden had a large sum of money laid out without a lease and hardly the promise of one. The question is one of the most difficult to deal with, but where there is a good feeling between landlord and tenant I don't think any Act of Parliament can- be necessary, and it is very difficult to frame an Act of Parliament which will govern these parties if they are determined not to work harmoniously together. If it is the intention of the landlord to take every advantage of a tenant's outlay, and if, on the other side, it is the intention of the tenant to take every legal advantage of a landlord, it is almost impossible to frame a good Act of Parliament, but as I trust that the great majority of the landlords of England are blessed as I am, with a tenantry who are willing to work with them, I hope and trust that the new Act of Parliament will not be worked hard, and that the landlords and tenants of England will be an example to all landlords, to show how class and class can work happily and harmoniously together. I am, I am afraid, going this winter to foreign climes and into countries where landlords and tenants do not work so harmoniously together as in this happy country. We have one foreigner here and I wish we had more, to see how happily we all work together. I beg now before I sit down to drink your very good healths, and with the toast I couple the name of Mr. Richards of Glascoed, who lives in the house where my ancestors came from, the house where Sir William Williams lived. I believe many generations of Mr. Richards's family lived there, though I am afraid I cannot reach back beyond his mother, whom I recollect thirty or forty years ago. I give your healths, coupled with the name of Mr. Richards.

Mr. RICHARDS—I hardly know why I should be selected to return thanks except as representative of a family which has lived under the Wynns for over a hundred years, but I can assure Sir Watkin that the kindness and hospitality he has extended to us this day will never be forgotten by us. It will be spoken of in many a home for many a year to come—the way we have been received in this noble mansion. It has been a very great treat to me, and I may, I think, say the same on behalf of every tenant, when I thank Sir Watkin for his hospitality to-day.

Mr. W. JONES (Gwrgant), London—Although not a tenant farmer I am descended from a long line of tenant farmers, maternal and paternal, for generations, and it is with the greatest possible pleasure that I am present at this gathering. It is one of the most delightful scenes I have ever witnessed in my life to see a happy tenantry with a happy landlord—Sir Watkin with us again; may he long remain in the same position. My toast is the health of Lady Williams Wynn and the Misses Wynn. Mr. Jenkins was going to take this toast into his hands, but the duty has fallen upon me. I know Lady Williams Wynn's perception, excellent judgment, and probity in performing the high duties of her high position. Her benevolence, charity, good sense, and everything that is necessary to make a good wife to Sir Watkin, all you who know her are aware of. I am delighted to see present Lady Williams Wynn, Lady Williams, of Bodelwyddan (his sister), and to see his daughter—this is a scene one may wait a long life to witness.

Mr. W. W. E. WYNNE, of Peniarth—I believe I am one of the olden time; few here indeed, I believe, are more of the olden time, or can recollect Wynnstay longer than I can. I remember the old birthdays year after year, but I never saw such a scene as this. You will hardly believe me, but I was born before the death of Sir Watkin's great grandmother, the widow of one who succeeded to the estates in the year 1719. Of course, I do not recollect her, as I was a very small child when she died, but I was born two years before that time. With each successive generation I have stood on intimate terms of friendship, and never have I been more intimate, I am happy to say, than at the present moment. Mr. C. W. W. Wynn told you just now he believed he was about the oldest officer in the yeomanry—why, I remember him when he was a baby in his cradle. I do not know much more that I have to say, but that I rejoice to see you here, and that, on behalf of Lady Williams Wynn, I thank you sincerely for drinking her health.

Sir WATKIN—I will now give the health of one who has been a kind friend to all. He is nearly related to me, and was one of those gentlemen asked to bring my estate into order and to try and create a good feeling between my tenants and me. I am sorry he is not here, but age will tell—age will injure the strongest man's health. Unfortunately, therefore, though his wife and sons are here, he, I am afraid, is on a bed of sickness, and cannot be amongst you. Still he takes a great interest in this meeting. I beg to give you the health of Sir Hugh Williams, Lady Williams, and their sons.

Captain WILLIAMS—I thank you for the kind way in which you have drunk the health of my father, whom old age has prevented attending here. I believe he is personally known to the greater part of those present, and, therefore, nothing would have given him greater pleasure than to have met you here as in the old time.

Sir WATKIN—Now that Sir Hugh has retired from the management of my estates, my friend Mr. Owen Slaney Wynne has undertaken the duties. He is known to you all, and I will not, therefore, take up your time with any panegyric. I will only say that he is a Welshman, and a gentleman, and I trust he is just. He is very zealous, and tries as much as he can to act fairly between landlord and tenant.

Mr. O. S. WYNNE—I am sure the way Sir Watkin has spoken of me is most gratifying. During the four years I have had the honour of representing Sir Watkin, I have had nothing but kindness from all present, and what would otherwise be a most difficult task has been therefore rendered pleasant. I sincerely trust that as long as I have the management of his property I shall be able to give satisfaction to Sir Watkin, and also to you, which will be my most earnest endeavour. There has already been very great improvement in the property, and I hope it will continue, and that it will benefit Sir Watkin as much as it will benefit you. I sincerely trust you will always remain friends.

PENNILLION

A ganwyd gan yr Awdwr, gyda chymeradwyaeth mawr,

YN Y WLEDD YN WYNNSTAY, HYDREF 29ain, 1875,

Er anrhydedd i

Syr WATKIN WILLIAMS WYNN, Marchog.

———

Yn mhlith yr holl foneddwyr,
  A geir yn Nghymru lân,
Mae rhai boneddwyr mawrion
  A'r lleill yn od o fân ;
Ond gwnewch un bwndel anferth
  O fonedd Cymru 'nghyd,
Syr Watkin, brenin Cymru,
  Sy'n fwy na rhai'n i gyd.

Lle bynag tyfa glaswellt,
  Lle bynag t'w'na haul,
Fel tirfeddiannwr hynaws
  Ni welwyd un o'i ail ;
Mae'n frenin gwlad y bryniau,
  A chyda hyn o ran,
Mae'n frenin yn nghalonau
  Ei ddeiliaid yn mhob man.

Ewch at y weddw unig,
  Ewch at amddifad tlawd,
Syr Watkin yw eu noddwr,
  Syr Watkin yw eu brawd ;
Trwy ddagrau diolchgarwch
  Ar ruddiau llawer un,
Argraffwyd yr ymadrodd—
  Syr Watkin ydyw'r dyn.

MYNYDDOG.

WYNNSTAY AND THE POETS.

WELSH Bards and English Rhymesters have vied with each other to do honour to the family of Wynnstay on all occasions of special interest.   One of the oldest compositions we have met with refers to the Denbighshire Election of 1741-2, the "Election Mawr" we have already alluded to, at which the rival claims of Wynnstay and Chirk Castle were set at rest.   This "poem" is preserved at Wynnstay, and is written underneath a well-drawn caricature crowded with figures.   In the picture the election itself is supposed to be depicted, and we have on one side a Bishop, and Walp—e with mitre in hand, Sir Watkin standing behind him, and beneath the words " By road from St. Asaph to Canterbury."   On the opposite side there is a 'lean soldier' driving pigs before him, and behind him a man creeping into a kennel, saying " I brother vote for brother George." This "kennel," or rather pig-stye, is fast being converted by another man into a house, by the building of a chimney, so as to form a residence for a voter.   Under the pig driver are the words " To a fair market— The Court."   Many of the characters are supposed to be uttering election cries, such as " I the Cobbler object against that vote for Sir Watkin !" " Has Sir W. Bagot power to make leases ?"   " Burn the Spy in the hand."   " I will call the Sheriff of this riot and he will adjourn the poll, " &c.   In one figure the " Chorister of St. Asaph " is represented, and there are several others that no doubt were significant at the time the cartoon was drawn.   The following are the verses :—

> "*Oh Liberty ! Oh Virtue ! Oh My Country !*"—CATO.
>
>   Who's that lucky Wight in the front doth stand
>   A Mitre in one—Borough in t'other hand ?
>   That's Walp—le who's to translate the Bishops ;
>   And Wyn—e for Denbigh Borough set up.
>   With Bribes and Promises Courtly doing
>   Endeavours the Country Party's ruin.

L

See the Bishop who sets us by the Ears
 Promotes those nor God nor Devil fears,
Wicked as Price or Tam'lain the better
 For his Election Schemes the fitter.
He'll have Vicars choral and Choir'sters poll'd,
 Tho' perjur'd—must swear they have a Freehold!

See, there a Soldier, so thin and so fine,
 Like the Devil runs after the herd of swine;
Oh! the Col—l but drive them from their sty,
 Builds chimney—A Voter their place to supply.
By Tricks like this Poll'd Resiants most
 Then of his Interest Braggs and Boast.

See there a mean Placeman behind Sir Bob
 Tom Breet—n with money election to job,
Has made George a Member (must give him a pension)
 By Williams out Poll'd to's Return no Prevention.
I'll Return him said Llo'd else sure ruin appears
 Behind the Bum Bailiff scratching his ears.

See there in Arms the Soldiers at Caerwis
 Snt Asap and Ruthin—does the Sheriff fear us
Or are they so near as against a known law
 That Coward to support? the Electors to awe?
Disappointed they'll be Watkins mob does no harm
 He's too wise—to the Captain said Griff'h of Garn.

See one near the Shrine with a thick folio book
 That's Paint'r who every Freeholder's name took;
Of all not taxt for forty shillings took notes
 Was of Them and non-Resiants destroying the votes.
This Pool—late a foot—n a Justice is made,
 Such justices as our Country Betray'd.

Who's that so Busy and Bigg in the Booth
 Demands Leases and pittles instead of the Oath?
That is Mr. Sher'ff—you some trick this delay
 All he Polls in a week might be Poll'd in a day.
But mangre his Queries the Castle's out done
 Sir Watkin has Freeholders two to his one.

Quoth Griff—h what then? I know Will:—and will burn
 If (tho Watkin they choose) He dont Castle return
Return'd as he causd at this Borough and Flint,
 Zounds! He'll stick at nothing—so there's nothing in't.
Perjur'd!—Informer! Lets secure his Retreat
 Then give him a Bond, and he'll give Jack the Seat.

> The Poll being ended the Courtiers did stare
>   To hear Mr. Sheriff the numbers declare :
> Thirteen hundred fifty-two for Watkin told,
>   Nine hundred thirty-three for Middleton Pooll'd;
> Of these old Freeholders two to one
>   For Sir Watkin ; most clergy for to did own.
>
> Then Justice he promis'd Sir Watkin to do
>   And made a Return in a day or two,
> According to Conscience and t'oath he had taken
>   He said—but he did not—for had he forsaken
> The 'Squire he'ad drawn in had quite been undone,
>   So the Castle return'd at all risques to be run.

Another bit of verse relating to the first Sir Watkin—when " The Honour'd Mr. Watkin Williams Wynn,"—refers to his election as Mayor of Chester, and is taken from the *Gentleman's Magazine* for 1736 :—

> Behold the man without ambition great,
> In all that's worthy man, the man compleat,
> Tho' rich not covetous, tho' great sincere ;
> Not proud nor servile, but in honour clear.
> No fawning flatterer, nor fashion's fool,
> Nor cheating gamester, nor the statesman's tool.
> A will unfeign'd ; a brave yet humble mind,
> The lover and the love of human kind.
> Who is not glad if such a man there be ?
> Who is not glad that WILLIAMS WYNN is he ?
> Amidst corruption, luxury and rage,
> Yet one true Briton shames a vicious age.
> Health, plenty, pleasure, round his table wait,
> And charity expands his friendly gate.
> Thou true exception to the general rule,
> Of wealth heap'd on the vile, the vain, the fool,
> Without hypocricy, here reigns confest,
> The honest zeal in the bold patriot's breast.
> Yet worthless wretches brand a patriot's name,
> His glory lies in what these wretches blame.
> Mark well, ye great ! that rise by servile ways,
> Who has more friends ?   Yet these his virtues raise.
> Brave Chester's May'r, how am I pleas'd to see,
> That so corrupt an age can relish thee !
> All : hail the Magistrate : their voices raise
> To thy desert ; even Cook himself does praise.
> The worthy May'r, lo, every breast has charm'd,
> Envy's appeas'd, and prejudice disarm'd,
> Proceed, brave WILLIAMS ! let us yearly see
> Some action good and great and worthy thee.

Our next poetical offering relates to a wedding, and it has evidently formed a portion of the stock-in-trade of an old Ballad-monger. The verses are printed on the commonest of paper and in the rudest of type, and at the top there is a coarse wood-block representing a short youth in breeches joining hands with a tall female in a hat. He stands in a respectful attitude, and the truly rural locality of the scene is marked by a solitary daisy of monstrous proportions growing on the sward at the backs of the loving couple. The original is preserved at Wynnstay, and it no doubt alludes either to the coming-of-age of the second Sir Watkin or to some festivity at Wynnstay in his time :—

BUMPKIN'S WEDDING.

A Favourite Song.

Bumpkin.

Take example from me, & be Married sir *Wat*,
I'm Bumpkin your Tenant from Salop,
Took Jenney to Church only yesterday morn,
And we've rode to Wynnstay on full Gallop.

CHORUS.

Sing Hey for a Wedding, sing hey for a Wife,
If you meet with a good one there's no fear of strife.

Jenny.

So much we have heard of this great Masquerade,
That we've come with the rest to be shew'd,
But first I got married for fear of mishap,
For in Masks th're so apt to be rude.
Sing hey, &c.

Old Thomas.

Old Martha and I for our souls could not stay,
Whilst our Children were all on the Ramble,
So packed up our Budgets & trudged it away,
To try our good luck in the scramble.
Sing hey, &c.

Martha Jallop.

Here's Cake from the Wedding to place in your Bed,
You'll dream of delights without measure,
Drawn thrice through the Ring this wonderful charm
Turns fancy to realized Pleasure.
Sing hey, &c.

Lubin.

Tho' I've just lost my Wife, I could not stay at home,
And miss the fine things at the Wedding,
We drank down the day, then the young ones at Night,
Threw the stocking and danced at the Bedding.
Sing hey, &c.

Jenny.

> Long life to sir *Wat*; success to *Wynnstay*,
>   But forget not his Elegant Mother,
> Like his ancestor happy, correct in his choice,
>   Kind Heaven produce such another.

CHORUS.
> Sing hey for a Wedding, sing hey for a Wife,
> If you meet with a good one there is no fear of strife.

The following speaks for itself. It was sung at a Public Dinner given to the father of the present baronet at "The Eagles Inn, Wrexham," on his return from the Continent after Peace was declared. The author was Richard Llwyd, the "Bard of Snowdon." The dinner came off March 18, 1815.

Tune '*Rule Britannia.*'

> Whate'er can swell the Patriot breast,
>   Or bid the Hero's heart rejoice,
> We bring—his country's high behest,
>   His bright award—her grateful voice.

CHORUS.
> With pride we meet—devote this day
> To *Wynn*, his country's friend and *stay*.
>   Rule Britannia, &c.

> His sires we find in firm array,
>   (And Time the regal record brings)
> Firm in Cambria's doubtful day,
>   And o'er her spread their eagle wings.

> Again in Favor's fostering hour,
>   They join'd the bold, the faithful band,
> That check'd th' encroaching plan of Power,
>   The Guardians of their native land.

> May heaven long grant this leading race,
>   From Mona's chieftain great and sage,
> Thy roofs Rhiwabon long to grace,
>   To bless—as erst—each future age.

> We see him like a Prince, preside,
>   His breast with Britain's welfare glow,
> The Powers of Emulation guide,
>   " 'Tis Reason's feast—the Soul's gay flow."

> Bid Science and the Sons of Toil,
>   With chaplets deck her honor'd choice;
> Bid Plenty laugh on Culture's soil;
>   " The hills exult, the vales rejoice."

His worth the milder Virtues sung
  In Charity—St. David's dome;
The ardent choral triumph rung—
  His grateful country's " welcome home."

The Orphan's praise—the Widow's prayers,
  Is Virtue's high and valued treat;
Its heaven—the soul ascending shares,
  It soars, when man is good and great.

The Brave, that glory bade to burn,
  From hostile fields and Britain's foes;
Shall now to tranquil scenes return,
  On Cambria's parent breast repose.

Whate'er can swell the Patriot heart,
  Or bid the Hero's breast rejoice,
We bring—to crown their high desert,
  Their honor'd country's cheering voice.

CHORUS.
With pride we meet, &c.

The next that we have to present to our readers is from the youthful pen of an ardent Welshman who, since he wrote it, has been engaged for half a century in active literary and theological labours. The lines were published in 1827, and refer to a summer evening's visit of the father and mother of the present baronet to the Vale of Llanbrynmair :—

Why now, my native vale! in bloom so gay?
Why art thou dress'd in living green to-day?
While groves and fields and purling streams combine
To form a prospect more than half divine.

Why dost thou now such smiling aspect wear?
Why does such fragrance fill thy healthful air?
Why sing thy birds around on every tree?
Their tuneful notes, in sweetest melody?

" My beauties thus, in graceful order meet
To cheer my passing ' LORD ' whom now I greet:
And Tempe's blooming charms are lent me—while
I'd fain return his LADY'S gracious smile."

Long live in bliss, this honor'd happy pair,
Adorning Virtue's cause, with pious care!—
Let joy attend their OFFSPRING's peaceful sway,
That—when all nature's beauties fade away—
The WYNNS, like stars, may shine, in realms of endless day.

SAMUEL, *Bryn-Mair.*

The last we have to offer is a gem in its way, and is preserved, in manuscript, as a curiosity, in Lady Williams Wynn's Scrap Book. Although undated it bears internal evidence as to which Sir Watkin it is intended for :—

ELEGY ON SIR W. W. WYNE COMING OF AGE.

A worthy Branch from Wynsday having attaind the age of twenty-one,
His late noble Parent deeds no doubt by he will be done—
Then his loving subjects will thrive, as have done afore,
With pelf in plenty—and cwrw dda in each floor.
> Long live Sir Watkin where ever he be
> The oftner he visits the Cymry the more attach'd they'll be.

The late noble Barronet was a Warrior, both courageous and Brave,
In Paddys land by his manovers, the Ancient Brittons did save ;
Should the friends of late Michael Murphy be ankcious of such contest again,
A young Branch of Wynsday will mount his steed, and over they will reign.
> Long live Sir Watkin, &c.

The late Nobleman was liberal, both generous and free,
At charitable institutions, none compared to he—
God send the young Nobleman health, than we will find,
A friend to the needy—halt, lame, and blind,
> Long live Sir Watkin where ever he be
> The oftner he visits the Cymry the more attach'd they'll be.

On the next two pages we give—for comparison and contrast—the amount of victuals consumed at Wynnstay when the second Sir Watkin came of age in 1770, and when the present Sir Watkin came of age in 1841. We should remark that in the former case the whole was disposed of in one day, whereas in the latter a whole week was occupied in the consumption.

COMING-OF-AGE IN 1770.

The following list of articles consumed at the Wynnstay Banquet, April 19, 1770, when the second Sir Watkin attained his majority, is taken from an old manuscript :—

30	Bullocks, and	60	Barrels Pickled Oysters
1	,, roasted whole	1	Hogshead Rock Oysters
50	Hogs	20	Quarts Oysters for Sauce
50	Calves	166	Hams
80	Sheep	100	Tongues
18	Lambs	125	Plumb Puddings
70	Pies	108	Apple Pyes
51	Guinea Fowls	104	Pork Pyes
37	Turkeys	30	Beef Pyes
12	Turkey Poults	34	Rice Puddings
64	Capons	7	Venison Pyes
25	Pea Fowls	60	Raised Pyes
300	Chickens	80	Tarts
360	Fowls	30	Peices of Cutt Pastry
96	Ducklings	24	Pound Cakes
48	Rabbits	60	Savoy Cakes
15	Snipes	30	Sweetmeat Cakes
1	Leveret	12	Backs Bacon
5	Bucks	144	Ice Creams
421	Lbs. of Salmon	18,000	Eggs
30	Brace of Tench	150	Gallons of Milk
40	Brace of Carp	60	Quarts of Cream
36	Pike	30	Bushels of Potatoes
60	Dozen of Trout	6,000	Asparagus
108	Flounders	200	Kidney Beans
109	Lobsters	3	Dishes of Green Peas
96	Crabs	12	Cucumbers
10	Quarts of Shrimps	70	Hogsheads of Ale
200	Crayfish	120	Dozen of Wine.

There was a very great quantity of Brandy, Rum, and Shrub.
Salt Butter cost £36, besides Fresh Butter.
Rockwork, Shapes, Landscapes, Jelly Blanc Manges, &c., &c.
A great quantity of Small Pastry.
One Cask of Ale that contained 26 hogsheads.

Three coaches full of Cooks were sent from London on ye occasion.
By computation 15,000 People all at ye same time dined in Sir Watkin's Park.

COMING-OF-AGE IN 1841.

The following is a list of articles consumed at Wynnstay during the week ending September 12, 1841, when the coming-of-age of the present Sir Watkin was celebrated :—

21	Oxen	30	Quarts of Prawns	30	Quarts Cherry Water
146	Sheep	7	Quarts of Pickled Shrimps for Sauce	164	Quarts of Ices
12	Lambs			141	Pine Apples
12	Calves	14	Pike	445	Lbs. of Grapes
6	Porkers	28	Tench	2,136	Peaches and Nectarines
12	Calves' Heads	10	Carp		
26	Sets of Calves' Feet	24	Eels	1,200	Apricots
6	Sets of Ox Feet	2	Trout	85	Melons
135	Pickled Tongues	2	Perch	3,100	Pears
10	Flitches of Bacon	2	Stags	3,450	Eating Apples
5	Westphalia Hams	17	Bucks	12	Bushels of Apples for Tarts
4	Strasburgh Hams	11½	Sacks of fine Flour		
6	Cumberland Hams	55	Measures of Wheat, Ground	180	Lbs. Filberts
25	York Hams			10	Bushels of Plums
3,608	Eggs	464	Lbs. Butter	22	Forbidden Fruit
28	Turkeys	226	Lbs. Lard	5	Bushels Currants
14	Geese	444	Quarts of Milk	206	Cucumbers
40	Ducks	207	Quarts of Cream	15	Bushels French Beans
701	Fowls	8	Cheese		
122	Pigeons	51	Hogsheads of Ale	15	Bushels of Peas
204	Grouse	17	Hogsheads of Beer	48	Bushels of Potatoes
21	Black Game			10	Bushels of Turnips
400	Partridges	829	Bottles of Sherry	8	Bushels of Carrots
27	Wild Fowl	558	Bottles of Port	560	Heads of Lettuce
69	Hares	294	Bottles of Claret	1,000	Heads of Celery
48	Rabbits	336	Bottles of Champagne	5	Bushels of Parsnips
267	Lbs. Turtle			8	Bushels of Spinach
280	Lbs. Salmon	56	Bottles of Maderia, &c.	4	Bushels of Sorrel
189	Lbs. Soles			10	Bushels of Onions
124	Lobsters	648	Bottles Soda Water	12	Bushels of Horse Radish
192	Whiting	72	Bottles of Brandy, &c.		
23	Turbot			120	Artichokes
18	Cod Fish	84	Bottles of Milk Punch	46	Bushels of sundry other articles from the Gardens.
180	Cray Fish				
8	Barrels of Oysters	112	Quarts of *Ponche a la Romaine*		
15	Bladders of Oysters for Sauce	54	Quarts Lemonade		

M

LETTERS AND ANECDOTES, &c.

THE following Facts and Fancies concerning Wynnstay and the Wynns are gleaned from various sources, and arranged as nearly as possible according to their respective dates.

OLD-FASHIONED MANNERS.

Under this heading Mr. Hayward, Q.C., in his extracts from the *Diaries of a Lady of Quality,* gives a letter from the first Sir Watkin (when Mr. Watkin Williams) written to his father at the instigation of Sir John Wynn, of Wynnstay. The "Diaries," we should state, were the work of Miss Frances Williams Wynn, the lady we have previously mentioned as being thrown out of a pony carriage when driving with her brother from Wynnstay to Nant-y-belan. The following is the passage : see page 295 of the work :—

"Sir William Williams, my great-grandfather, seems to have been addressed by his children and dependants with much more respect than we have lately seen evinced in writing to the Queen. The tutor to his sons always writes from Oxford of my grandfather as *My Master,* of his brother as *Mr. Robert,* and addresses Sir William as *Your Honour.* In 1714 my grandfather writes for Sir J. Wynn, ' He has desired me to acquaint you that, if you approve of it, he would be highly glad if you could meet us at St. Albans to conduct us into town, for he is the most apprehensive of danger betwixt that place and London of any ; he is by no means for my staying in London any longer than the Mellins are delivered, and if possible, to return to Barnet or Highgate that night, but hope, Sir, you will send him word that it is not practicable for me to return sooner than the Monday following, suppose we come in Friday or Saturday night. The noise of our going is spread all about the country, and somebody has told him that Prichard the Highwayman is gone abroad, which makes him under ye greater concern, so would gladly have returns for some parte. Dear Sir, your ever dutiful Son, WAT. WILLIAMS.' "

The " Mr. Robert" mentioned here was at the time of his death in 1763 Member for the County of Montgomery, and Recorder of Oswestry. He owned Erbistock Hall, now a part of the Wynnstay estate, and a considerable extent of property in the parish of Mallwyd, most of which now belongs to W. W. E. Wynne, Esq., of Peniarth.

Mr. Richard Williams, of Penbedw, another grandson of The Speaker and Attorney General, was Mayor of Owestry in 1747, during the period that his brother Robert was Recorder ; and his son, Watkin Williams, was Mayor in 1770. Richard Williams was Member for the Flint Boroughs, and married Annabella, daughter and heiress of Charles Lloyd, of Drenewydd, Esq. ; he died in 1759. His son, Watkin Williams, at one time represented Montgomeryshire, and afterwards the Flint Boroughs. He was Lord Lieutenant of the Counties of Denbigh and Merioneth, and died in 1808.

THE FIRST SIR WATKIN MAYOR OF CHESTER.

We have given some account, on an earlier page, of the gay doings at Chester when the Honour'd Mr. Watkin Williams Wynn was chosen mayor. We are informed that under the old corporation of the city the Mayor had the right to nominate a Freeman during his year of office, and an entry in the Corporation books, fol. 79, under date, Jan. 11, 1736, states that—

"At the same Assembly npon Mr. Mayor's Recommendation, It is unanimously ordered that John ffoulkes of Eriviot, Esqre., be admitted a freeman of this City gratia."

The Mr. John Ffoulkes here mentioned was great grandfather of W. Wynne Ffoulkes, Esq., County Court Judge of Cheshire, and we believe that gentleman by right of descent has been admitted, and has voted as a Freeman of the City.

FESTIVITIES AT CHESTER WHEN THE SECOND SIR WATKIN WAS MAYOR.

The following letter is addressed by Miss Baldwin (afterwards Mrs. Thelwall, of Llanbedr) to her sister, Mrs. Townshend, of Wineham, then with her husband, Col. Townshend, in Ireland.— W. W. Ff.

Hoole, Octr. 27th, 1773.

My dearest Sister,

What a strange void does a great Festival make; the hurry and bustle is. all over. Sir Watkin is Mayor. . . . . I must begin with Saturday, I went and dined at the Heskeths, and went to the play, which was bespoke by Sir Watkin "Much ado about nothing," and "Harlequin's invasion." The House-crowded. Lady Williams was very unbecomingly dressed—her hair without powder; and her cap, which was edged with Diamonds, not half an inch from her forehead,. which is remarkably high. She is a fine woman, her complexion natural and beautiful roses and lilies. Sunday we went at nine o'clock with a large party to see the Feast. But it was nothing extraordinary. Beautiful Temples and ships of paste;

but no sweetmeats of any sorts or Jellies &c. &c. or anything to make a desert eatable. There was as Rigbye informed me four courses of meat at Dinner and a hundred and forty Brace of partridges and everything in proportion. Above three hundred people dined at the Exchange. Monday at seven we went to the Exchange, which was quite full. Lady Williams was a very brilliant. She looked very handsom and the picture of good nature and happiness. Her gown was something of gold but I don't know what. She had a fly cap entirely of Diamond with the wings bent down close to her forehead. A finer necklace than Lady Grosvenor's, earrings watch and chain all Diamond a stomacher with four Bows each of four Bows all Diamonds so that she was quite dazzling. Her Bracelets were pearls and she had a row with a large drop falling below her necklace, which was the princess Dowager's and cost five hundred guineas. She was valued at £20,000 pound exclusive of her inestimable self. She is with child so did not dance. The room was hotter than the furnace of Shedrek Mechack and Obednego, but Sir W.'s servants broke all the windows and revived us. Lady W. sat in the middle of the Court of Justice with all the fine Ladies on each side of her and on the Table all sorts of cakes and wines &c. &c. We began to dance country dances at nine o'clock. Two full sets from top to the bottom. I danced with Foster Cunliffe.   .   .   . Tis much the fashion to bring your partners nosegays and Mr. Cunliffe brought me a large one of Myrtle. At twelve we went to supper, which was all cold but soups. All sorts of fruit and wines and everything was conducted with ease propriety and elegance. Sir W. own servants waited. Eight in green and silver liveries and four in ruby coats and blue and silver waistcoats. All the twelve in bags and some had wigs on. We danced after supper till near three and Sir W. coach was ready to take the company to their own houses so that every thing was elegant. The room was lighted with hundreds of coloured lamps as it was at the masquerade and there was a Temple at supper supported by forty pillars and from one pillar to the other were festoons with little coloured lamps and the middle was raised very high and little lamps hung round where bells are hung on a Chinese Temple. The effect was beautiful. The Militia band play'd during the entertainment. There was above five hundred people in the room, but of different ranks, from dazling stars at one end to little heads eclipsed in block bonnets at the other. Mrs. Cholmondeley was very fine. Her gown dark and trimed with Brussels, a deep flounce &c. &c., and very fine jewells,

.   .   .   .   Your sincere and faithful friend,

                                   MARY ELIZTH. BALDWIN.

LLANFYLLIN RACES.

The great carnival of the year, at Llanfyllin, last century appears to have been the race week, which included the wakes, June 28. The races were held on Cefnbran, where are still visible the remains of a vast number of "tafarnau tywyrch"—huts of sods, where cakes, drink, &c., were sold. They were attended by the elite of the county and by hundreds of spectators. Sir WATKIN WILLIAMS WYNN presented a cup, value £50, to be run for, a large prize in those days, and this, with other good stakes, brought hither horses of some repute. There was a grand stand on the course, given, it is said, by Sir Watkin, which was carried away to Tan-y-foel, one of his tenements, when the races were transferred to Cyrn-y-bwch near Oswestry, about 1790. A party of strolling players acted each night of the race week in the town hall, and parties and enjoyments were the order of the day.—Rev. R. WILLIAMS, M.A., Rector of Llanfyllin, in *Montgomeryshire Collections*, 1870.

"SIR WATKIN'S SAVIOUR."

Mr. T. G. Jones, of Llansantffraid, writing of that parish in the Transactions of the Powysland Club, (vol. 4, p. 124) says :—" We have but few monuments of interest to note. The first that we come to is one within the narrow railing and known as 'Sir Watkin's Saviour': the person buried here was a John Deakin, of Gelly, known locally as Captain Deakin, he having joined the volunteers mustered by Sir WATKIN WILLIAMS WYNN to quell the rebellion in Ireland." Sir Watkin, as leader of the volunteers, incurred the deadly hatred of the Irish; and many are the tales told of the attempts openly and by stratagem made to take away his life: amongst others it is related of John Deakin that, whilst riding near to Sir Watkin during the heat of a skirmish, an Irishman raised his sword, and would have " cut off Sir Watkin's head," had not Deakin, with a quicker hand, taken off the head of the Irishman! Just at that moment Sir Watkin, turning round, called out, " God bleth me, John, watth the matter?" pointing to a most dangerous wound in the abdomen, Deakin had received from the Irishman's sabre. How he was cured and sent home to Llansantffraid we are not told.

INSCRIPTIONS ON THE VASE

Presented to Sir WATKIN WILLIAMS WYNN on his return from France in the year 1815 :—

To Col. Sir Watkin Williams Wynn, Bart., the patriot leader of his brave countrymen during the rebellion in Ireland and invasion of France, as a memorial of his repeated voluntary services, the county of Denbigh presents this tribute of esteem and gratitude. 1815.

Viro ingenio W. W. W. Baronetto, Cambriensium suorum, in domestica tantum stipendia conscriptorum, sed ipso hostante premium in Hibernia pro legibus imperii Britannici: mox et intra Galliæ fines pro publica Europe salute marti voluntaris militantium commilitoni præfectoque in patriam feliciter reduci Denbighenses unanimes. 1815.

> Y fail arian am filwrio—roddwyd
> I raddol fwyn Gymro,
> Syr Watkin Brigin ein bro,
> I'w gyfarch a'i hir gofio.

" It cost 19s. 6d. per oz., and measured 3ft. 2in. by 2ft. 4in. across, and contained 14 gallons."

LUDICROUS SCENE AT CALAIS.

In July, 1815, " the summons having come (to Lady Castlereagh to meet Lord Castlereagh, at Paris), Lady Castlereagh and I (Lady Emma Edgecumbe) lost no time in starting on our journey. We found Sir Watkin Williams Wynn and his brother, Mr. Henry Wynn, at Dover waiting for a passage, which Lady Castlereagh gave them in the packet she had engaged. When at Dessin's at Calais the authorities came to pay their respects and make fine speeches to Lady Castlereagh, and in the middle of this somewhat formal proceeding, Sir Watkin's chair broke under him with a crash, and down he went to the ground. The authorities expressed great distress, and helped to pick up the prostrate Baronet, while Lady Castlereagh and I could, I fear, scarcely refrain from laughing."—*Reminiscences of a Septuagenarian*, page 24-5.

EARLY ANTIQUITIES OF WALES.

In September, 1823, as we are informed by the *Archæologia Cambrensis*, vol. 1, p. 242, and other records, a Gold Torque was found by Mr. James Hughes of Machynlleth, son of the late rector of Dolgelley, whilst grouse shooting upon the boggy margin of Llyn Gwernan (the Alder-tree Pool) near the northern cliffs of Cader Idris. He observed part of a circular rim above the surface of the ground, which upon drawing out and finding it perfect in its form, he carried home and actually offered to a friend for five shillings as a curiosity, but the offer being rejected he gave it to Mr. David Jones, of the House of Commons, with a view of ascertaining what it might be, not supposing it valuable. The latter gentleman recognized it to be an ancient Welsh Torque. It was afterwards purchased by Sir WATKIN WILLIAMS WYNN, father of the present baronet, for £50, and is now treasured up at Wynnstay. It measures forty-two inches long, and weighs eight ounces and eight pennyweights; the intrinsic value of the gold being £36. The third vol. of the *Montgomeryshire Collections* contains a drawing of this interesting antiquity of the Principality.

SIR WATKIN'S SHAKESPEARE.

Dr. Dibden in his *Library Companion*, published in 1824, says :—" Mr. Grenville informs me that an ancestor of Sir WATKIN WILLIAMS WYNN had a copy of the first folio Shakespeare UNCUT. It was lying on the table in that condition, when, in a luckless moment, a stationer (in the neighbourhood of Wynnstay) came in. The book was given by him to be bound; and OFF went, not only the edges, but half of the MARGINS!!! O unprecedented act of bibliopegistic barbarity! No wonder, on my mentioning this anecdote to Charles Lewis, that his teeth were set on edge, and he gave an involuntary inward groan!"

BIRTHDAY ALE.

It is said that when the present Sir WATKIN WILLIAMS WYNN was born, 200 measures of malt were used for the beer brewed on the occasion, and that the whole was tapped when he came of age. Mr. W. Martin, the cellarer (who had been forty-eight years at Wynnstay), and Sir Watkin, drank the first jug between them. The Martin family had been in the same service for nearly two centuries.

SIR WATKIN'S DELIGHT.

This beautiful old melody was originally called " Y Veillionen " or, The Trefoil, and was a great favourite with the first Sir WATKIN; hence it became known among minstrels, who visited Wynnstay during their *clera* seasons, as Sir Watkin's Delight. Near Beddgelert there used to be an old mansion called Meillionen, and it remains there yet for anything I know. This air is known in that part of Wales as " Consêt Gwraig Meillionen," or the Lady of Meillionen's Conceit. It has also been known as " Y Veillionen o Veirionydd " and " Yr Hen Veillionen." In the dancing days of the Principality this air had a great run as a hornpipe; it is nevertheless, when played slowly, one of the most elegant and flowing melodies. The late John Parry *(Bardd Alaw)* wrote one of his most beautiful and happiest variations to it. When the first daughter of the present baronet was born my dear old friend Talhaiarn wrote, I believe, suitable words for the occasion upon this air in English and Welsh. Mr. Owen Alaw arranged the music. The air only is published in the second part of the " Gems of Welsh Melodies."—J. C. H.

HARD WORK.

A " Brother" having an appointment to meet Sir WATKIN WILLIAMS WYNN, at Wynnstay, on Masonic business, he arrived a few minutes before the hour named—three p.m.—and right glad he was to get shelter from the fury of the storm outside; he was told that Sir Watkin had crossed from Kingstown to Holyhead during the previous night, had slept a couple of hours at Chester, and then posted to Wynnstay, where he had partaken of a hasty breakfast, and gone cub-hunting. " And," continued the informant, " Sir Watkin won't have much time to give you, for he only calls here to dress, as he is going to Brynkinalt to dinner." Now, to an ordinary mortal, a rough passage from Kingstown to Holyhead would have been a laudable excuse for spending the day in bed; but when manly sport is before him, the baronet of Wynnstay is not an ordinary individual. And Sir Watkin, although so fond of sport in the field, is generally in at the death at St. Stephen's. We have known him hunt all day in Denbighshire, and ride to Ruabon station in hunting costume, in time for the five o'clock evening express train for London, dress himself on the journey—a good two hundred miles—and vote with his party the same night.

PRINCE OR DEVIL?

As we leave Llanuwchllyn we at once enter into a wild moorland, which, as we pass on, becomes enclosed by high and rugged hills, and along this somewhat desolate-looking valley we travel (on the banks of the Wnion) for a dozen miles, until we approach Dolgelley. There is little calling for remark on the way. One funny story is suggested as we slacken for Drwsynant Station, which is told of Sir WATKIN WILLIAMS WYNN, in the old coaching days. A tourist of an inquiring turn of mind joined the coach at that place on its way to Bala. Inside he found a stout gentleman enjoying a nap. When he awoke, the tourist asked whose was the farm they were passing. " Mine," was the reply, and the gentleman again slept. Another wakeful moment, and another question: " Whom may that mountain belong to?" "To me;" followed by another doze. Again came a wakeful moment, and the question, " Do you know who is the owner of that valley?" with the answer, " I am not sure, but I think most of it's mine." No more questions were asked, but when the coach reached Bala the tourist bolted into the hotel, saying—" I have been riding with either a prince or the devil." "You are right," replied a native. "You have been riding with the Prince *in* Wales and a devil-ish good landlord!"—*Gossiping Guide to Wales.*

"PLEASE GOD AND SIR WATKIN."

The devout aspiration of the patriotic Welshman may, we hope, see its fulfilment in the case of the most recent example of munificence on the part of the Lord of North Wales. Sir WATKIN WILLIAMS WYNN has, we learn, resolved, with the assistance of his friends and neighbours, to found an " Accident Hospital" at Ruabon, taking the cost of the building upon his own shoulders, and leaving the expense of maintenance to be defrayed partly by subscription and partly by payment on the part of the patients. The object of the hospital is to furnish, in case of accident, prompt surgical aid and experienced nursing, thus supplying a want long felt in Ruabon, where accidents in connection with mining operations and the management of machinery are of frequent occurrence.—*Lancet*, Dec. 22, 1872.

The following belong to no precise date, so we conclude our chapter of anecdotes with them.

HISTORICAL PARALLEL.

In a pamphlet published in 1841 at the *Chester Courant* office, and detailing the festivities consequent on the coming-of-age of Sir Watkin Williams Wynn, we have the following :—

" Sir William Williams, the first baronet, married Miss Kyffin of Glascoed, in consequence of pleading her father's cause in an effectual manner at the Assizes for the county of Salop."

" Pompey the Great in pleading before the Prœtor Antistius pleased him so much that he gave him his daughter Antistia in marriage."

The writer gives Plutarch as his authority for the latter statement, and our readers will find, on an earlier page of this book, some reference to the " cause " which was no doubt in the mind of the writer in the *Chester Courant.*

WELSH MÈRLYNS.

Sometime, about the reign of Queen Anne, we are told, there was introduced into Wales a galloway called *Merlin*, who became the sire of a celebrated stock of Welsh Ponies. Up to that period the breed was degenerating, and the only name the Welshman had to describe his little mountain steed was *Ceffyl Bach*. And thus, it is said, an ancestor of Sir WATKIN WILLIAMS WYNN introduced at the same time an important race of ponies to the mountains and a new word to the vocabulary of Wales.

SIR WATKIN'S PUDDING.

There are few public dinners held in North Wales where the bill of fare does not include "Sir Watkin's Pudding." It will probably surprise many of our readers to know that this rich dainty was not called after any of the Wynnstay family at all, but is said to have been the " delight " of a " Sir Watkin " who was an alderman of London.

THE WYNNSTAY MANUSCRIPTS.

THE disastrous fire at Wynnstay in 1858 destroyed the whole of the Library, including the following Manuscripts, &c., the list which we copy being one sent by Miss Angharad Llwyd to the Welshpool Eisteddfod in 1824 :—

" *Cofrestr o Law Ysgrifau Cymreig Mr. William Morys, Cefn y Braich, hynafiaethydd enwog,* yr hwn a'u gwerthodd i Syr William Williams, Bar., Llanforda, am 70*p.*, a'r hyn sydd yn weddill o honynt a geir yn Wynnstay, palas Syr Watcyn Williams Wynn, Bar., A.S."

Brut y Brenhinoedd, folio, 6 inches deep.
Brut y Tywysogion, folio, 6 inches.
Cyfraethau Howel Ddâ, lib. 1, 8 inches.
Arvau Cymru, folio, 6 inches.
Aborigines Britannicæ, written by Mr. Wm. Morys, large folio, 7 inches.
Theobardicon, sef Duwiolgerdd, folio, 6 inches.
Y Basilico Bardicon, sef Brenhingerdd, folio, 8 inches.
Aristiobardicon, sef Boneddgerdd, folio, 8 inches.
Miscellanea, sef Brithlyfr, rhan i., folio, 4 inches.
Ibid. rhan ii., folio, 4 inches.
Archiobardicon, sef y Llyfr dû o Gaerfyrddin, folio, 8 inches.
Neobardicon, sef Diweddargerdd, folio, 8 inches.
Logobardicon, sef Cyfrinach Beirdd Ynys Brydain, folio, 8 inches.
Proverbia, Latine et Wallice, per Dr. Wm. Davies, folio, 6 inches.
Antiquarium Britannicum, Repertorium Britannicum, folio, 2 dig,
Gildas Nennius Eulogium, Britannicæ Insulæ, folio, 4 dig.
Chronica a Cadwaladro rege ad Leolinum ult., folio, 3 inches.
Dau lyfr Cywyddau o law John Jones o Ysceiviog (Gelli lyvdy), allan o lyfrau Simmwnt Vychan, y ddau yn un, folio, 6 inches.
Adversaria Historico Britannica, per Wm. Morys, folio, 2 inches.
Lectionarium sive Spicilegium variorum Lectionum, Scriptum per William Morys folio, 4 inches.
Llyfr Gwyn o Hergest, folio, 4 inches.
Cywyddau o destynau y Salmau, folio, 1 inch.
Thesaurus Cornucopiæ, o law Mr. William Morys, folio, 1 inch.
Cywyddau o waith Ed. Wrien, folio, 3 inches.

N

Britochronicon ar hên femrwn, quarto, 4 inches.
Hen Lyfr Duwiol, un Lladin, ar hen femrwn.
Cyfraith y Cymry ar femrwn, folio, 3 inches.
Cymmydau Cymru, folio, 4 inches.
Buchedd y Saint, yn Saesnec, ar femrwn, 4 inches.
Primitivæ fidei, venerabilis liber, scriptum in pulchrâ manu, et initium uniuscujusque partis incipit cum aureâ literâ.
Collectanea Latina, scripta per William Morys, folio, 5 inches.
Chronological Essays, by William Morys, 1660, folio.
Llyfr Cywyddau o waith amryw, o law Mr. William Morys.
Index ad Codicem Hoelianum, by Mr. Wm. Morys, folio, 1 inch.
Talin o Gyfraith y Llysoedd ar femrwn, folio, 2 inches.
Anthropopathy, in English, by William Morys, folio, 9 inches.
Bardorum Britannicorum Grammatica autographo membranaceo, fideliter transcripta, per Gul. Mauricum, Lansiliensem.
Observations on the Scriptures in English, by Mr. William Morys.
Llyfr Cywyddau o waith amryw Feirdd, folio, 3 inches.
Chronicon Asseri Menevensis Episcopi, fideliter scriptum e Vetusto Codice Archiepiscopi, Math. Cant.
Florilegium, written in English, by William Morys, in 1641.
History of Bellinus and Brennus defended, written by Mr. William Morys to Mr. R. Vaughan, of Hengwrt.
Llyfr Prawf eneid, folio, 1 inch.
De Britannica et primis ejus hominibus, per William Morys.
Awdlau i Dywysogion Cymru, o law Dr. Powel, quarto, 2 inches.
De Descriptoribus rerum Britannicarum, per William Morys, folio, 3 inches.
The Life of St. Edmund, in verse, written by William Morys.
Llyfr Cywyddau o waith T. Prys, o Blas Iolyn, folio, 4 inches.
Chronologia Britannica, written by William Morys.
Llyfr meddiginiaeth o waith Meddygyn, quarto, 5 inches.
Llyfr Phisigwriaeth, folio, 5 inches.
Llyfr Achau ag Arfau, o law Simmwnt Vychan, quarto, 2 inches.
Cywyddau o waith Dd. ab Gwyllym, quarto, 4 inches.
An old MS. Psalter, in vellum, 4 inches.
Llyfr Clera Rhys Cain, folio, 4 inches.
Another old Psalter, with great golden letters on vellum, folio, 3 dig., William Morys.
Brut y Brenhinoedd, or the History of the Kings of Britain, being a copy of the original which Jeffrey of Monmouth transcribed into Latin.
Brut y Tywysogion, being a continuation of the British History by Caradog of Llancarvan. A copy of the original which Humffrey Llwyd translated into Latin, and Dr. Powell into English.
Index ad Leges Hoëli Boni, being a summary of the heads contained in the Welsh Laws. A chronicle beginning with Æneas, and an old Extent of Oswestry, folio, 8 inches.
Y Llyfr Dû. First, it contains the most ancient poems that probably exist in our language, Taliesin, &c. Second, a large collection of ancient prophecies, Merlin, Robin Ddu, &c. some of which are curious. but the greater part are forgeries, as to the names and pretended expositions of Merlin. Prophecies written probably about the time of the conquest of England, and adapted to the hopes of Ancient Britons, from Owen Gwynedd, Owen Glyndwr, and Henry VII. Third, Computatio Manuale,

or Manual of Computation for the regulation of the Calendar, written by Dd. Nanmor. This is very interesting, as giving the names of the Saints in the Welsh Calendar, about A.D. 1450. It is drawn up in the same manner as the computation of John De Sacro Bosco (or John of Holywood), but the writer quotes a book written by Alcharbitius, some of whose works are supposed to be in the Bodleian library. Fourth, The Medical System of the Physicians, taken principally from Hippocrates and Pliny. Fifth, Dares Phrygius, a loose and incorrect translation from the Latin.

John Salusbury, of Erbystoc's celebrated Book of Pedigrees, which appears to have been commenced by Thomas Salusbury, of Erbystoc, about the year 1640, and to have been carried on with many additions from his son, John Salusbury, down to the year 1671, illuminated and in high preservation, folio, 2 inches deep.

Welsh Pedigrees, compiled by John Salusbury, of Erbystoc, folio, 2 inches.

Welsh Pedigrees, including those of Cheshire and Shropshire, old writing, folio, 4 inches.

Organum Britannicum, being a Catalogue of Authors treating of the History of Britain, written in Welsh, Latin, and English, by William Morys, 1659, folio, 2 inches.

Antiquarium Britannicum, written by Wm. Morys, in 1659.

Miscellanies, a thin folio, not perfect.

An Account of the Mayors of Chester, and a History of England, by Robert Ince, Coroner of Chester, in 1639, thin folio, not perfect towards the end.

A brief Declaration of the first inhabitants of this island's lineal descent from Brutus, by Olyver Mathews, in 1671; it ends with the Kings of England. English, a thin folio, perfect.

An Account of Parliaments, holden in Richard III.'s time. English, folio, 1 inch deep, not perfect.

Thomas Skinner's Petition about the Shipping in 1667. English, a thin folio.

Laws of Howel Dda. This volume contains annotations by Camden. A portion of the Apocalypse in Irish, with a translation on part of the leaves. Transcript of MSS. of Mr. Vaughan of Hengwrt's Pedigree by Mr. David Parry, folio, 3 inches.

The Pedigrees of Cwmmwd Maelor, written in the time of Sir Richard Trevor, of Trefalyn, folio, 4 inches.

Graphiologia de traditione Genealogica Britan. Giraldus Cambrensis, &c., written in 1670, folio, 6 inches.

An old copy of Brut y Brenhinoedd with clasps, interleaved with notes, by Mr. William Morys, quarto, 3 inches.

A Latin History, and at the end a copy of a Welsh MS., given to Lord Carew by Mr. Owen, 1609, containing a History of the Marches of Wales, a few pedigrees, quarto, 3 inches.

Volume containing the Poems of Dd. ab Edmund, Gutto'r Glynn, Gyttyn Owain, Howel ab Dd. ab Inn ab Rhys, Iolo Goch, Lewys Mon, Dr. Sion Cent, Tudyr Aled, &c., finished in 1605, by John Jones, of Gelli lyvdy.

Brut y Tywysogion, written by John Jones, of Gelli lyvdy, while in the Fleet Prison in 1636.

Brut y Tywysogion, from 680 to 1332, written by William Morys, from the Hengwrt copy.

Brut y Tywysogion, begins differently from the one transcribed by William Morys.

A folio cover, full of old miscellaneous letters.

Norton de Alchemia, folio, 1 inch.

Miscellanies, written in 1773. This volume contains the Ystym Colwyn Pedigree, folio.

Barddoniaeth, with Achau brith rhwng Taliesin a Myrddin, in the handwriting of William Morys, folio, 5 inches.

Hen gerdd Lyfr, written by William Morys, in 1660.

Encyclopædia Bardica, written by William Morys, folio, 5 inches.

Pregethau a wnaeth Maistr Latimer, ag a bregethodd gar bron yr Arglwyddes Catrin, Duges o Suffolk, yn oed yr Argl. 1552, transcribed into Welsh by Roger Pulston.

A Treatise on Wales and the Marches, account of fees paid, &c., written in 1723, folio, 1 inch.

A general Collection of all the Offices in England, with their fees, written in 1595, folio, 1 inch.

Proffwydoliaeth a Prydyddiaeth Merlyn, a Barddoniaeth by different bards, mostly Dd. Llwyd, written in Charles I.'s time, quarto, 2 inches.

A volume of Miscellanies, containing poems by Lewis Glyn Cothi; Annals of Owen Glyndwr; Account of the Lordship of Oswestry; Welsh Antiquities from the Triads, &c.; return sent to the Commission sent by Henry VII. into Wales, to inquire into the Pedigree of Owain Tydyr; Account of Wales and the Families; Genealogical Extracts from the Pryse MSS; Manner of keeping the Parliaments, &c., quarto, 4 inches.

Volume containing Pedwar mesur ar hugain, Henwa'r Siroedd, Cymmydau, &c., written in Henry VII.'s time; this volume has W. Morys's name inside the cover, dated 1650, quarto, 4 inches.

Chronicle of the Welsh Princes, of the Kings of Europe, and of the Popes of Rome, in Latin, octavo, 1 inch.

Heraldry, mostly Welsh Arms, illuminated, and some little notice taken of the families entitled to bear them, the Fifteen Tribes, rudely executed in 1597, quarto, 3 inches.

Another thin quarto of Welsh Heraldry, and Pedigrees, with the Arms well delineated, and coloured.

Reports of the House of Commons in 1673, English.

A folio of English Laws.

Adversaria Historica, &c., contains " Henwa'r Llyfrau Cyfreitheu yr hên Fritaniet a mesur Tervyneu a gwerth crosseu, John Jones." The extent of the Lordship of Oswestry. A Cowydd recited at Cnockyn Castle, when Syr R. Cynaston received the Order of Knighthood from Edward IV., King of England.

A Catalogue of Hengwrt Library, written 30 years ago. The last catalogue finished by Mr. Robert Vaughan, in 1661, after his library had received considerable additions, especially the books of Mr. John Jones, of Gelli lyvdy, cannot be found as yet. It was in the hands of Dr. Ellis, of Dolgellau, when William Morys was last at Hengwrt. The substance of the above is taken from a note in William Morys's handwriting, without date, quarto, thin.

A Catalogue of Mr. William Morys's books, folio, 1 inch.

Another of Mr. Williams Wynn's, taken in 1729.

A small box, half a yard long, and about 4 inches deep, full of interesting miscellaneous papers, written by Edward Llwyd, Account of Places, and some of the Cambrian Superstitions.

Scriptor Rerum Brit. Adversaria Graph. Miscell., all Welsh, many places marked with the year 1605; it contains Llyfr Clera Rhys Cain, folio, 4 inches.

Hen Farddoniaeth, copied in 1694, folio, 4 inches deep, many blank leaves towards the end.

" Llyfr Dared Cymraeg, scrifenedig o lyfr Risiart ab Sion o Llanganhaval, yr hun a goppiassi yntai o lyfr Simmwnt Vychan, John Jones, 1605. Ag o'i un yntai a gaed scrifenydd William Morys, 1664." It begins with Llyma Ddysg i adnabod cerddoriaeth cerdd dafod, herwydd Llyfr Dd. Ddu, Athraw, folio, 4 inches.

Cywyddau ymryson rhwng Edmwnd Prys, Archiagon Meirionydd, a William Cynwal, copied by William Morys in 1669, folio, 3 inches.

Barddoniaeth Bedo Brwynllys, Sion Wyn, Huw Arwistli, Sion Ceri, Ieuan Deulwyn, &c., old writings, quarto, thin.

Miscellanies quarto volume, thin.

Dd. Nanmor's Poems, Thomas Pryse, and Simmwnt Vychan.

Dosparth Edeyrn Dafod Aur, y pedwar mesur ar hugain, &c.

Comments upon the Scriptures, by John Salusbury, of Erbystoc, written in Welsh, in 1668, a thin quarto, not perfect.

Miscellanies, written by William Morys. This volume contains Welsh Prophecies, translated into English, folio, thin.

The Legends of the Saints, in English verse, and written upon vellum, folio, 2 inches.

Volume containing Judge Doddridge's cases, English.

Charta 9, 10, &c., of Edward II. yn y Twr, Latin, concerning Wales, with occasional remarks, written in Welsh, quarto, 3 inches.

A copy of some papers communicated by Dr. Hudson, A.D. 1705. Observations made by a traveller, quarto.

A Memorandum Book concerning Oliver Cromwell's Rebellion in Wales, giving Castles that capitulated, &c., written from 1638 to 1647, English. This volume also contains catalogues, Chronological, Historical, Britannicorum, &c.

A Catalogue of my Lord Bangor's MSS. in his study, taken June 1696. Cynval's Book of Pedigrees is among them, and also the Laws of Howel Dda, &c. Likewise six MSS. contributed by the Rev. Dr. Jones, Dean of Bangor, written by Mr. Williams, schoolmaster of Beaumaris school, about 1670, all concerning Wales.

A Specification of the Charter of Howel Dda, from a copy taken from the White Book of Hergest, by Peter Roberts.

An interesting Memorandum Book, written between the years 1664 and 1668, by a gentleman in the Navy Office, who was a cousin to Mr. Andrew Thelwall, of Llanrhydd, and Mr. Thelwall, of Plas y Ward.

Taliesin, and other Barddoniaeth, bound up with an old Latin MS. upon vellum, octavo, 2 inches.

Prayers and Poems, on vellum, English, a few of the first pages lost.

Llyfr Sion Watcyn, Jun., on vellum, 1. inch thick, with William Morys's name inside the cover, 1664.

Latin Herbals, written in 1626, and another of the same size, containing a Dictionary of Plants, both octavo.

Cywyddau allan o'r Llyfr Gwyn o Hergest, weithian, sef hen femrwn, llyfr a scrivenwys (folio mawr) yn amser Edward y Pedwerydd, Frenhin Loegyr, omnia per amanuensem exemplificivi ego Gwil. Maur. Llansilin.

SIR WATKIN'S CRUISE AND RETURN.

SOON after the Banquet, already recorded, Sir Watkin, Lady Williams Wynn and their daughters, with Miss Cocks and Mr. Bennett, left Wynnstay for a cruise in the Mediterranean; and we have been courteously supplied, by Captain Jones, with the following Log of the *Hebe*, Sir Watkin's Yacht, and description of the vessel.

The *Hebe* is an iron screw steam yacht of 350 tons, and she was purchased by Sir Watkin from Charles McIver, Esq., of the Cunard Co. Her crew consisted of eighteen hands, all told, besides a stewardess, viz. :—Capt. Rowland Jones, commander; Mr. Rothwell, chief officer ; Mr. Burkill, second officer ; Mr. Mason, chief engineer ; Mr. Miller, second engineer ; Henry Rome, chief steward ; William Ainsworth, second steward ; Daniel McCally, cook ; Thomas Wynn, cook's mate; Walter Rome, A.B. ; Joseph Bennet, A.B. ; Patrick Murphy, A.B. ; James Thomson, A.B. ; Alfred Lockyer, A.B. ; John Crabbe, A.B. ; John Jones, fireman ; John Wynn, fireman ; William Williams, fireman; Mrs. Smith, stewardess ; and Thomas Yates, valet.

Nov. 8, 1875.   Weighed anchor at 6 a.m. and steamed to sea.—6-45, Rock Light-house abeam.—8, passed the Formby Light Ship.—8-20, set fore and aft sails.—8-30, over the Bar.—9-30, North-west Light Ship.—11-30, Great Orme's Head, and took in all sail. Showery, with strong wind and head sea. At Noon, Point Lynas, bore W, N, ¼ N, 8 miles.—2-40, passed between the West Mouse and the Skerries.—3-40, rounded inside Holyhead breakwater. — 4, anchored in 7 fathoms.   Passengers—Simon Yorke, Esq., and Mr. and Mrs. Owen Wynne, who all left the yacht here.   Distance from Liverpool 68 miles.

Nov. 9.   3-40 p.m., weighed anchor and steamed to sea.—9-30, Bardsey Island abeam 6 miles.   11-25, Cardigan Bay Light Ship abeam 8 miles, strong breeze.

Nov. 10.   8 a.m., St. Anne's Head abeam.—8-45, anchored off Milford town.—11-40, steamed up to New Milford and took in coals.   Distance from Holyhead 110 miles.

Nov. 11.   Remained in port.

Nov. 12.   12-30 p.m., weighed anchor.—3-30, set fore and aft sails, strong breeze, 6-20 p.m., the Bishop's Light abeam 8 miles.—11 p.m., took in all sail.

Nov. 13. Strong breeze, rain, and rough sea. 2-30 p.m., fresh gale.

Nov. 14. Fresh gale and high sea.

Nov. 15. Moderate wind, all sail set. 10 a.m., took in all sail, sighted land.

Nov. 16. Moderate breeze, overcast.—4-45 p.m., Cape Finisterre abeam 4 miles.

Nov. 17. Light airs and thick.—9 p.m., Cape Roca abeam 7 miles.—6-30 a.m., sighted Cape St. Vincent.

Nov. 18. Strong breeze, rough head sea.—10 p.m., sighted the Cadiz Lighthouse. Distance 9 miles.

Nov. 19. Fresh breeze, clear.—3-10 p.m., Cape Trafalgar abeam.—10-10 p.m., passed Europa Point.—10-40 p.m., anchored at Gibraltar. Distance from Milford 1,115 miles. Took in coals.

Nov. 20. 6-45 p.m., weighed anchor, calm and clear.

Nov. 21. 11 p.m., Cape Palos abeam.

Nov. 22. Moderate wind and rough sea.

Nov. 23. Strong breeze and rough sea.—9-30 a.m., made the land.—At 1 p.m., arrived at Marseilles. Distance from Gibraltar 682 miles. Remained in Marseilles until

Dec. 9. 8 a.m., Sir Watkin and Lady Williams Wynn and family came on board. —4-35 p.m., unmoored ship and steamed out of harbour by N.E. entrance, wind W.— at 4-55 p.m., rounded the Dilon Light Ship, fresh breeze and cloudy.

Dec. 10. Strong breeze and head sea, ship rolling very much.—1-20 p.m., rounded Nice breakwater and dropped anchor. Distance from Marseilles 110 miles.

Dec. 11. Remained in port.

Dec. 12. Weather bright and clear, in port.

Dec. 13 and 14. In port.

Dec. 15. 2-30 p.m., weighed anchor, sea moderate, clear weather.

Dec. 16. 9 a.m., arrived at Ajaccio. Distance from Nice 130 miles.

Dec. 17. 6-30 a.m., weighed anchor, weather moderate and cloudy, set the fore trysail.

Dec. 19. Light breeze and cloudy. 10-15 p.m., rounded Palermo breakwater.— 11, arrived in harbour. Distance from Ajaccio 320 miles.

Dec. 20, 21, and 22. In port.

Dec. 23. 10-35 a.m., weighed anchor, bound for Malta.

Dec. 24. Light wind and fine weather. 6-15, Marsala abeam.—10-25 a.m., slowed engines and entered Valetta harbour.— 10-40, anchored. Distance from Palermo 215 miles.

Dec. 25. Christmas Day. North wind, dull weather.

Dec. 26 to 29. In port.

Dec. 30. Moderate breeze and clear weather, took in coals.

Dec. 31. In port, weather showery, with vivid lightning, took in 3½ tons of water.

Jan. 1 to 4, 1876. In port.

Jan. 5. Brisk breeze, cloudy.—7-30 a.m., unmoored ship.—11 a.m., weighed anchor and steamed to sea, bound for Corfu.—11-20 a.m., passed Valetta lighthouse.

Jan. 6. Strong breeze, cloudy.—6-40 p.m., Cape Passaro light abeam 5½ miles.— 10-31 p.m., rounded Syracuse Harbour light, and anchored in 6 fathoms.

Jan. 7. 8-15 p.m., weighed anchor.

Jan. 8. Moderate and cloudy, set fore and aft sails.—Midnight fresh and overcast.

Jan. 9. 7-50 a.m., arrived at Corfu, and anchored off the Citadel in 14 fathoms. Distance from Malta 370 miles.

Jan. 10. Moderate breeze with rain, in port.

Jan. 11. Moderate gale, dark rainy weather, in port.

Jan. 12. Fresh breeze and cloudy.—6-30 a.m., weighed anchor.—10 a.m., set fore and aft sails, strong head sea.—Noon, fresh breeze with rough sea.

Jan. 13. Wind and sea increasing, took in both waist boats on deck.—9 20 p.m., hauled down the head of trysail, and slowed the engines.—Midnight, moderate gale and high sea.

Jan. 14. 7 a.m., hove the ship to.—Noon, fresh gale with squally dark weather, at this time ship was only making 2 knots ahead and 2 knots lee way, wind S.E. to S.S.E. This was the heaviest gale of wind the *Hebe* was in, the Captain never left the deck for 24 hours, during which time the ship was hove to, with the engines going dead slow ahead.

Jan. 15. Moderate and fine, ship making 8 knots.—4 p.m., sighted the Gozo light, W.N. ¼ N.—7 p.m., entered the Quarantine Harbour, moored to buoy in Sliema Creek. Distance from Corfu, 370 miles.

Jan. 16 to 23. Light breeze and fine weather, in port.—Took in coals.

Jan. 24. Moderate breeze and dull weather.—10-15 a.m., cast off from the buoy and steamed to sea, bound for Gozo.—12-10 p.m., arrived at Gozo.—3 p.m., weighed anchor and steamed back to Malta. Distance from Malta to Gozo and back, 36 miles.

Jan. 25. Moderate and dull in port. The reason the yacht was kept so long at Malta was owing to the serious illness of Miss Mary Nesta Williams Wynn.

Jan. 26. Fresh breeze, cloudy, cast off from the buoy 10 a.m., bound for Syracuse.—6 p.m., Cape Passaro abeam.—9-5 p.m., entered Syracuse Harbour. Distance from Malta, 84 miles.

Jan. 27. Wind E.S.E. light breeze, dull sky, in port.

Jan. 28. Light breeze, dull.—3 p.m., weighed anchor bound for Zante.—Midnight, sharp breeze.

Jan. 29. Brisk breeze and cloudy.

Jan. 30. Moderate and cloudy, ship going 9 knots.—11 p.m., Argostoli light, N.E. 12 miles, arrived at Cephalonia. Distance from Syracuse, 260 miles.

Jan. 31. Light breeze and fine weather.—12-10 p.m., weighed anchor, strong breeze and clear weather.—1 p.m., ship going 9 knots.—5 p.m., anchored inside Zante breakwater. Distance from Cephalonia, 36 miles.

. Feb. 1. Moderate gale and clear, in port.

Feb. 2. N.E. wind, strong, with clear weather.

Feb. 3. Fresh breeze and clear weather.—9-55 p.m., weighed anchor.

Feb. 4. Moderate weather.—6-20 p.m., passed Peros light.

Feb. 5. Moderate breeze and fine weather.—3.30 p.m., arrived at Athens. Distance from Zante, 243 miles.

Feb. 6. Moderate breeze and cloudy weather, in port.

Feb. 7 to 12. In port.

Feb. 13. Light wind and fine. 6 a.m., weighed anchor.—8 a.m., set fore staysail and trysail.—3-20 p.m., arrived at Milo, and anchored in 7 fathoms. Distance from Athens 80 miles.

Feb. 14. Light breeze, fine weather. 6 a.m., weighed anchor. — 2-10 p.m., arrived at Santorin. Distance from Milo 55 miles. 5-30 p.m., steamed out to sea again, passing out by the Volcano and south end of Thirasia Island.

Feb. 15. 5 a.m., rounded Cape Sidara.—7-30 a.m., anchored off the town of Palaio Kastrio, on the east-end of Crete, for shelter. Noon, light wind with thunder and lightning.

Feb. 16. 2-40, weighed anchor and steamed to sea, bound for Alexandria.—6 p.m., squalls of rain, hail, thunder and lightning.

Feb 17. Fine clear weather, smooth water. Midnight, sighted Alexandria light, and slowed engines.

Feb. 18. 6 a.m., steamed into the harbour. Distance from Santorin 390 miles. Strong breeze, cloudy. 8 a.m., hauled her into the graving dock for the purpose of cleaning and painting ship's bottom.

Feb. 19. Moderate and fine weather. 8 a.m., floated ship and hauled out of dock.

Feb. 20 to 24. In port, coaled the ship.

Feb. 25. Moderate breeze and fine weather. 3-30 p.m., weighed anchor and steamed out of harbour.—11-35 p.m., Cape Boorlos light abeam.

Feb. 26. Moderate breeze, clear weather, ship going 10 knots, course S.E.E. ¼ E. —3-40 a.m., Damietta light abeam 7 miles. 5 a.m., sighted Port Said light.—7 a.m., anchored in harbour. Distance from Alexandria 143 miles.

Feb. 27. Fresh breeze, cloudy. 5 p.m., weighed anchor, light wind, dull sky.

Feb. 28. Light wind and dull, daylight, sighted the Syrian coast. 7-35 a.m., anchored about 1¼ miles off the town of Jaffa. Distance from Port Said 132 miles.— 11 a.m., landed passengers and luggage. From here Sir Watkin, Lady Williams Wynn, and party, made an excursion to Jerusalem, the River Jordan, and the Dead Sea, living in tents. At three o'clock the yacht weighed anchor and steamed away for Port Said.

Feb. 29. Light airs and fine weather. 6-30 a.m., arrived at Port Said. Distance from Jaffa 132 miles.

March 1 to 10. In port.

March 11. Moderate breeze, fine weather. 5 p.m., weighed anchor and proceeded to sea.

March 12. Light breeze, fine weather. 9-10 a.m., anchored in 7 fathoms, off Jaffa. Distance from Port Said 132 miles. 3-15 p.m., family came on board again.— 3-30, weighed anchor and steamed for Beirut.—9, Cape Carmel abeam 5 miles, ship going 8 knots.—Midnight, calm, fine weather.

March 13. Calm, fine weather, course N.E., N, ¼ N. 12-30 a.m., Tyre light abeam.—2-45 a.m., Sidon.—5 a.m., Beirut. 6-30, anchored in 9 fathoms off the landing place. Distance from Jaffa 120 miles.

March 14. Moderate breeze, fine weather, at anchor.

March 15 to 18. In port.

March 19. Moderate and fine. 6-50 p.m., weighed anchor.—8, set trysail, wind S.E., course N.W. ¼ N. Midnight, fine.

March 20. Moderate and fine. 7 a.m., took in trysail.—8-20 a.m., anchored 4 fathoms off the town of Larnaka, in the Island of Cyprus. Distance from Beirut 110 miles. 2-30 p.m., hove short.—3 p.m , weighed anchor.—7-30 p.m., Cape Gata light abeam 1 mile.

March 21. Light airs, fine weather. At Noon the Takula mountain bore by compass N.E. by N.—4 p.m., passed the Island of Hypsili.—5-20 p.m., anchored in 5 fathoms at the head of Port Vathy. Distance from Larnaka 233 miles.

March 22. Calm and fine. 5-50 a.m., weighed anchor and proceeded along the coast.—8 a.m., anchored off the ruins of Patara. Distance from Port Vathy 26 miles. —10-20 a.m., weighed anchor.— 1-50 p.m., anchored off the town of Makry in 6 fathoms. Distance from Patara 26 miles.

March 23. Moderate and clear, wind N.W. 5-25 a.m., weighed.—10-30 a.m., anchored in Rhodes outer harbour in 4 fathoms. Distance from Makry 43 miles.

March 24. Fresh and clear, wind N.W. 6-5 a.m., weighed.—11-23, passed Cape Krio.—1-40 p.m., anchored at Boudroum off the Greek town in 5 fathoms. Distance from Rhodes 67 miles.

March 25. Light airs and clear weather. 5-25, weighed.— 6-45, anchored in the Roads at Cos in 5 fathoms. Distance from Boudroum 12 miles. 9-20, weighed anchor and left for Patmos.—1-20 p.m., anchored in Port Scala in 12 fathoms off St. John's Church. Distance from Cos 45 miles. 4-10 p.m., weighed.—6-40 p.m., anchored for the night in a small bay on the west side of Fourni Island. Distance from Patmos 17 miles.

March 26. 5-15 a.m., weighed and proceeded for Smyrna.—11-27 a.m., Pasha Island Lighthouse abeam 1 mile.—4-15 p.m., passed the outer Light Ship.—5-10 p.m., anchored in Smyrna harbour off the Marine Parade in 7 fathoms. Distance from Forni Island 115 miles.

March 27 and 28. In port.

March 29. Light airs and fine weather, coaled the ship and took in 4 tons of water.

March 30. Light breeze, fine weather. 2 p.m., weighed anchor,—3-30, passed the outer Light Ship.—6 p.m., anchored for the night in Fourges south harbour in 10 fathoms. Distance from Smyrna 32 miles.

March 31. 5-30 a m., weighed anchor.—8-50, passed the town of Mytylene.— 12-15 p.m., Cape Baba abeam 1 mile.- 2-40, Tenedos Island.—3-30, entered the Dardanelles, fresh breeze, clear.—5-45, stopped at Chanak for pratique.—6-15, proceeded. —6-30, rounded Point Nagara.—8-55, Gallipoli light abeam 1 mile.

April 1. Fresh and cloudy, wind E.N.E., course E. by N. ¼ N., ship going 8 knots.—3 a.m., passed the Island of Marmora.—10-30 a.m., rounded Seraglio Point.—11 a.m., arrived at Constantinople, anchored on the Pera side in 19 fathoms. Distance from Fourges 248 miles.

April 2 to 5. In port.

April 6. Moderate breeze, dull, cloudy weather.—10-20 a.m., weighed anchor and made fast to a buoy.—11, slipped the buoy and steamed up the Bosphorus. Noon, rainy, dark weather.— 1-45, turned and steamed back to Constantinople. Distance run, 40 miles.- 4 p.m., made fast.—5-30, slipped and steamed to sea.—5-40, Seraglio Point abeam.

April 7. Moderate breeze, misty weather.—2 a.m., Marmora Island abeam 3 miles.—6-45, Gallipoli light abeam, passed into the Dardanelles.—8-40, stopped at Chanak to board the Guard Ship.—9 a.m., ahead, full speed.—11, the east-end of the Island of Tenedos abeam, wind N.N.E., brisk breeze, fine weather, course S.W. ¼ S., ship going 10 knots.

April 8. 12-40 p.m., Cape Baba abeam.—4 p.m., set the fore trysail, rough sea, ship going 10 knots. – Midnight, Mandili Island abeam 1 mile.

April 9. 11 a.m., rounded Cape Malea.—Noon, Cerigo Island light abeam 3 miles, fresh breeze, fine weather.— 2-50 p.m., Cape Matapan abeam half a mile.—7 p.m., squally, wind moderate, head sea, ship going 8 knots.

April 10. 4 p.m., moderate gale, cloudy weather, ship going 10 knots.

April 11. Fine. 3-45 a.m., Cape Spartivento abeam 4 miles.—7-30 a.m., passed Mount Etna.—7-50, made fast to a buoy in Messina harbour. Distance from Constantinople 790 miles. 12-10 p.m., cast off and proceeded for Naples, light breeze, fine weather.—5-50 p.m., Stromboli Island abeam 11 miles, wind N.N.W., ship going 9 knots.

April 12. 4 a.m., sighted Capri light.—6-10 a.m., stopped close to Capri to visit the Grotto. —7-20, steamed for Naples.—8-30 a.m., anchored and moored, stem on to the breakwater. Distance from Messina 175 miles. Coaled the ship.—3 p.m., Sir Watkin left the ship for England.

April 13 and 14. In port.

April 15. Moderate breeze, dull weather.—11-15 a.m., steamed out of Naples harbour, bound for the Island of Elba —12-20, passed through the Procida passage. — Midnight, rainy, thick weather.

April 16. Moderate, unsteady breeze, with rainy, thick weather.—4 a.m., weather clearing.—6 a.m,, Giglio Island abeam 2 miles, wind S. to W., ship going 9 knots.— 10-20 a.m., anchored in Port Ferrago, in the Island of Elba. Distance from Naples 220 miles.—3-50 p.m., weighed anchor and steamed to sea.—9 p.m., Cape Corso light abeam 6 miles.—Midnight, fresh breeze, dark, cloudy weather, rough sea, ship going 7 knots.

April 17. Strong breeze, cloudy, rough sea.—2 a.m., set fore trysail, ship going 6 knots.—4 a.m., took in trysail, wind N.W., course N.W. ¾ N., ship going 5 knots.— 11 a.m., Villa Franca Lighthouse abeam 1 mile.—11-30, entered Nice harbour and anchored. Distance from Elba 144 miles.

April 18. Moderate and cloudy. 10 a.m., weighed anchor.—2-40, Cape Camarat abeam 2 miles.—5-30, the Grand Ribaud abeam.—7-20, entered in Toulon harbour opposite the dockyard in 5 fathoms. Distance from Nice 78 miles.

April 19. 5-50 a.m.. weighed anchor and steamed to sea.—6-5, passed the Light Vessel.—9-30, rounded Marie Island.—10-35 a.m., anchored at Marseilles. Distance from Toulon 45 miles. 2-30 p.m., Lady Williams Wynn and family left the yacht for England.

April 20. Moderate breeze, dull weather, coaled the ship. 9-30 a.m., weighed anchor.

April 21. Moderate and cloudy.—10 a.m., weighed anchor.—10-13 a.m., rounded the breakwater.—Noon, squally, with rain.—11-20 p.m., Cape St. Sebastian abeam 11 miles.—Midnight, fine, clear.

April 22. 10 a.m., set fore and aft sails.—Noon, moderate, showery, ship going 9 knots.—2 p.m., in all sail.—8 p.m , moderate and fine.— 10-50 p.m., Cape St. Antonio abeam 4½ miles, ship going 10 knots.

April 23. 4 a.m , brisk breeze.—7-25 a.m., Cape Palos abeam 3 miles.—Midnight, calm and clear.

April 24. 1-25 a.m., ship going 8 knots.—Noon, rounded Europa Point. Distant half a mile.—12-20 p.m., anchored in Gibraltar Roads in 4 fathoms. Distance from Marseilles, 682 miles.—4-30 p.m., weighed and steamed to sea.—7 p.m., passed Tarifa Lighthouse 1 mile.—9-30 p.m., Cape Trafalgar abeam 6 miles, ship going 9 knots.

April 25. Noon, Cape St. Vincent, bore N. by W. ¾ W. Distant 10 miles, wind N , course N.N.W., ship going 9 knots.—1 p.m., rounded Cape St. Vincent, 1 mile distant —10 p.m., slowed engines.—Midnight, fresh and breezy.

April 26. 3-40 a.m., steered in for the mouth of the Tagus.—4-40 a.m., received Pilot.—5-10 a.m., passed Fort Julian.—6-5 a.m., stopped for pratique.—7 a.m., anchored at Lisbon in the Man of War ground in 10 fathoms. Distance from Gibraltar, 300 miles.—4 p.m., coaled the ship.

April 27. 7 a.m., weighed anchor and steamed to sea in charge of Pilot.—8-20 a.m., discharged Pilot.—9-30 a.m., rounded Cape Roca, distant 2 miles, fresh breeze. —1-30 p.m., Cape Carvoeiro Lighthouse abeam 2 miles.—10 p.m., squally, ship going 9 knots.

April 28. 8 a.m., fresh breeze, cloudy, N.W. swell-reefed trysail and staysail.— 1-10 p.m., Cape Finisterre abeam 8 miles.—8 p.m , wind increasing with a heavy cross sea, wind W., course N.E., N. ¾ N., ship going 10 knots.—Midnight, fresh gale with squalls, reefed main trysail.

April 29. Noon, wind and weather the same.—4 p.m., wind and sea moderating. Midnight, moderate, cloudy, took in all sail.

April 30.   5 a.m., strong breeze with head sea, wind N.E., course N.E., ship going
6 knots —7 a.m., ship going 4 knots —Noon, strong breeze and head sea, ship going
2 knots —9·30 p.m , Bishop's Rock Light abeam, ship going 5 knots.—Midnight,
fresh, overcast, wind N.E., course E. by N., ship going 6 knots.

    May 1.   1·52 a.m., Wolf Rock Light abeam.—3·15 a.m., Longships, wind and
weather moderating, ship going 7 knots.—Noon, moderate breeze, fine weather.—2·45
p.m., Small's Rock Lighthouse abeam.—3·10 p.m., Grassholm Island.—3·45 St.
David's Head abeam half a mile.—8 p m., light breeze and fine.—11 p.m., Bardsey
Island Light abeam half a mile —Midnight, fresh and clear, ship going 10 knots.

    May 2.   2·5 a.m., passed South Stack.—2·50, Skerries.—4, Point Lynas.—5,
received Pilot.—8·15, crossed Liverpool Bar.—10, anchored off the Morpeth Dock.
Distance from Lisbon, 975 miles.—3·30 p.m., weighed anchor.—6 p.m., passed into
the Birkenhead Dock.—7·30 moored to the N. side of the W. Float.

The total distances run by the Yacht *Hebe* were as follows :—
Liverpool to Holyhead, 68 miles.   Holyhead to Milford, 110.   Milford
to Gibraltar, 1,115.   Gibraltar to Marseilles, 682.   Marseilles to Nice,
110.   Nice to Ajaccio, 130.   Ajaccio to Palermo, 320.   Palermo to
Malta, 215.   Malta to Corfu, 370.   Corfu to Malta, 370.   Malta to
Gozo, 18.   Gozo to Malta, 18.   Malta to Syracuse, 84.   Syracuse to
Cephalonia, 260.   Cephalonia to Zante, 36.   Zante to Athens, 243.
Athens to Milo, 80.   Milo to Santorin, 55.   Santorin to Alexandria,
390.   Alexandria to Port Said, 143.   Port Said to Jaffa, 132.   Jaffa to
Port Said, 132.   Port Said to Jaffa, 132.   Jaffa to Beirut, 120.   Beirut
to Larnaka, 110.   Larnaka to Port Vathy, 233.   Port Vathy to
Patara, 26.   Patara to Makry, 26.   Makry to Rhodes, 43.   Rhodes
to Boudroum, 67.   Boudroum to Kos, 12.   Kos to Patmos, 45.   Patmos
to Forni Island, 17.   Forni Island to Smyrna, 115.   Smyrna to
Fourges, 32.   Fourges to Constantinople, 248.   Up the Bosphorus
and back, 40.   Constantinople to Messina, 790.   Messina to Naples,
175.   Naples to Elba, 220.   Elba to Nice, 144.   Nice to Toulon, 78.
Toulon to Marseilles, 45.   Marseilles to Gibraltar, 682.   Gibraltar to
Lisbon, 300.   Lisbon to Liverpool, 975.   Total, 9,756.

During the few days the *Hebe* remained in port at Malta, early in
January, the Freemasons gave " The R.W.P.G.M. of North Wales
and Shropshire " a warm welcome at the Masonic Hall, Valetta.   Sir
Watkin's health was proposed, in eulogistic terms, by the R.W.D.P.G.M.
of the Province, and "hearty good wishes" were expressed by a
distinguished company of Brethren.

After an absence of nearly five months Sir Watkin reached London
on Monday morning, April 17, and proceeded to Wynnstay the same
night.

THE WELCOME HOME.

SIR WATKIN'S return on the evening of Monday, April 17, was too sudden for any very great demonstration on the part of his friends and neighbours at Rhuabon ; and had it been otherwise it was thought more fitting to include in the public welcome Lady Williams Wynn and family. But after an absence of five months it was not to be expected that the popular baronet would be allowed to return without the event's being marked by a " welcome " of some sort, and we are told that on the day of arrival " the hoisting of the British Standard on the church tower was a sign to the inhabitants of the Rhuabon district that something unusual was about to take place, and before long it was known that Sir Watkin was expected home by the 9 47 p.m. train. Long before that time a concourse of people congregated in and around the station. Sir Watkin, evidently being anxious to avoid any demonstration, quickly passed through the station door, accompanied by Mr. Owen S. Wynne. The crowd cheered lustily, and followed the carriage through the village to the park gates. The church bells rang merrily. Looking from the station the village presented a pleasing appearance ; almost every window was lighted up, whilst on the Wynnstay Arms sprays of gas in the form of WWW illuminated the whole village."

On the 25th of April the more public demonstrations took place. Sir Watkin and family arrived at Rhuabon station by an afternoon train, and found the village throughout so densely crowded with friends and well-wishers that there was scarcely room for their carriage to pass from the station to the park. On emerging from the station Sir Watkin was presented with an address from the inhabitants of Rhuabon. The Rev. Mr. Edwards, the Vicar, briefly stated that he was deputed to make the presentation, and handed the following address :—

To Sir Watkin Williams Wynn, Bart., M.P.—We, the undersigned, on behalf of the parishioners of Rhuabon, desire most sincerely to give you a very hearty welcome

P

on your return to your home in this parish, after what seemed to many your long absence. It would be needless to remind you of what you have seen yourself, not only during your recent illness, but on all occasions, how deep and personal an interest has ever been shown by the inhabitants of this parish in the joys and sorrows of the House of Wynnstay. It is therefore with special pleasure that we address you on this occasion. We could but sympathize with Lady Williams Wynn and yourself on the necessity you felt for leaving your home and occupations for the winter months to seek health in warmer climes. We admire your wise determination and patient endurance, and we now most sincerely congratulate you on the successful result of such journey, and we trust that with God's blessing your restoration to health may be complete and lasting. We pray that you may be spared for many years to your family, and that a life so valued, by not only your own immediate neighbourhood, but throughout the Principality, may long be continued and insured by every blessing both temporal and eternal.

> R. Chambres Roberts, F.R.C.S., Chairman, G. H. Whalley, George Edwards, William Jones, David Jones, Samuel Lewis, Robert E. Jones, E. Wood Edwards, vicar, A. L. Taylor, C. F. Jones, B.A., curate, Thomas Yardley, William Davies, H. C. Murless, treasurer, R. Lloyd, hon. secretary.

Mr. Whalley, M.P., read a leter from the Mayor of Wrexham, regretting his inability to attend. The hon. gentleman said it had been the wish of Lieut. Whalley and Captain Roberts that the Yeomanry and Volunteers should have been present, but owing to the great difficulties to contend with this had been abandoned.

In reply, Sir Watkin said he was happy to return to Wynnstay, and hoped to long live and remain amongst them. He regretted very much that the state of his health had compelled him to go amongst strangers—he had found the climate there much warmer than in Denbighshire, but he had wished to return home, where many still warmer hearts awaited him. He could only repeat to them Lady Williams Wynn's thanks and again himself thank them from his heart for their kindness.

Mr. Lloyd, of Ruthin, then presented an address from the Tenantry of that district, which was signed by Thomas Jenkins, Plasyward, John Denman, Glanrafon, Robert Edwards, Plascoch, William Lloyd, Well-street, W. J. Roberts, Well-street, Thomas Taylor, Wynnstay Arms, Hugh Jones, Garthgynan, W. Eyton Lloyd, Graig, Samuel Evans, Ty'ntwll, Thomas Roberts, Pentrecoch, Hugh Edwards, Well-street, Edward Davies, Well-street, Mary Evans, Caerfameth, Lewis Evans, Llanfair, Edward Roberts, Borthyn. Sir Watkin thanked Mr. Lloyd and his Ruthin friends, and a start was made for the lodge gates when another halt was made to receive an address, in Welsh, from Rhos. The Vicar of that parish, Mr. Jones, said that it was intended by the people of Rhos to erect a clock as a permanent memorial of the day Sir

Watkin returned to the district restored to health. Mr. W. Griffiths then read the address, which was signed as follows :—J. Jones, vicar, Cadeirydd y Pwyllgor. Aelodau y Pwyllgor : Joseph Griffiths, William Griffiths, Henry Dennis, Benjamin Davies, E. F. Fitch, John Wynn Jones, Joseph Evans, Thomas Owens, Sergeant Jones, Joseph Owen, John Owen, E. Lettsome, Daniel Evans, Robert Davies, Joseph Davies, Fred. Owen, Edward Tunnah, Owen Hughes, Hezekiah Jones, David Hughes, William Williams, Robert Roberts, Richard Hughes, Ezra Jones, John Griffiths, John Green; Geo. E. Woodford, Ysgrifenydd. Sir Watkin, in returning thanks, lamented that he was not able to address them in the tongue which prevailed in the country before the Saxon invasion.

Fifty or sixty stout fellows now took the horses out of the carriage, and drew it at a brisk pace up the avenue, the whole concourse following and shouting. The band of the 1st Denbighshire Rifle Volunteers, bandmaster, Mr. Jennings, marched in front playing " Home, Sweet Home," and afterwards, " Home from a Foreign Shore." Rhuabon was arrayed in flags, the bells rang out merry chimes, and towards Wynnstay house green and red bannerets were planted on each side of the drive. At its termination a fine arch had been erected by the gardener, Mr. Middleton. It was made of evergreens, mingled with primroses, daffodils, and rhododendrons, and on one side was lettered, " Welcome Home," and on the other, " Home, Sweet Home." Arrived at the house, Sir Watkin simply said, " I'm sure I'm much obliged to you," and with his family and friends got down. The children from Miss Williams Wynn's school, dressed in their picturesque red cloaks, were waiting to receive him, and the Rev. Studholme Wilson, the chaplain, on behalf of those present, again welcomed Sir Watkin home after his restoration to health, amid ringing cheers from all around. Sir Watkin said he could not say much more on a subject on which he had already spoken thrice. He trusted, however, they would allow him to thank them for the hearty welcome they had given him. Good old ale was plentifully served out, and the concourse did not disperse till late. At night Rhuabon was brilliantly illuminated.

At Bangor Steeplechases, on Friday, April 21, Sir Watkin was presented with an address by Lord Combermere on behalf of the Wynnstay Hunt. The ceremony took place at half-past two in the afternoon, and in making the presentation the noble lord said he had been deputed by the members of the Hunt and the occupiers of the land over which he and his friends had hunted for a period of thirty-five years, to make the presentation. The address, he was happy to say, was signed by over

1,000 gentlemen.   They were very desirous to express the satisfaction
they experienced in seeing him back from his Mediterranean cruise,
and restored to comparative health by his sojourn abroad.   His Lordship then read the address, which was as follows :—

To Sir Watkin Williams Wynn, Bart., M.P., April 21, 1876.

Dear Sir Watkin,—We, the undersigned, members of the Wynnstay Hunt, and
occupiers of land in your hunting country, desire to present this address of congratulation on your return home.   Your constant kindness and courtesy deserve our sincere
thanks and acknowledgment.   For thirty-five years you have with the greatest
liberality and success- entirely at your own expense—kept up your splendid pack of
fox-hounds and hunting establishment.   The sport you have shown has, we believe,
been second to none in that

> " Pastime for princes, prime sport of our nation,
>   All for enjoyment the hunting-field seek."

Helping also to maintain social harmony and good fellowship among all classes, your
genial presence has this year been greatly missed, and we truly rejoice to see you again
amongst us, and trust your health and vigour are restored, and that you may long
remain our honoured master—enjoying with Lady Williams Wynn and your children
the high position you now hold, and be, as hitherto you have been known—the friend
of all.

(Signed)   COMBERMERE, *Chairman.*

The address is a most costly and elaborate work of art, designed and
illuminated by Mr. E. B. Baker, Chester.   It is enclosed in dark green
morocco, with red morocco (Sir Watkin's colours) inlaid in a rich
border of elaborate gold tooling, with foxes' heads, whips, horns, caps,
&c., in each corner of the border; Sir Watkin's arms in the centre,
painted in gold and colour on ivory inlaid; on the reverse side the
initials W.W.W. elaborately worked out.   The book contains fifteen
leaves, three leaves devoted to the illuminated address, and twelve to
the subscribers' names.   On the first leaf, enclosed in a most chaste border,
are the full armorial bearings of Sir Watkin ; on the next page commences the address, enclosed in a very elaborate border, in the centre
on the top of the border, are the arms of Cadrod Hardd, a chieftain seated
in the Isle of Anglesey, at the commencement of the 10th century, who
had several sons, of whom Idhon ap Cadrod was ancestor of the Wynn
family, and his arms are on the left hand side of the border.   In the
bottom of the border is a water-colour view representing Wynnstay, the
principal seat of Sir Watkin, and on either side of this view the Arms
of Griffith ap Cynan, Prince of North Wales, who reigned fifty-seven
years ; also the Arms of Idwal Voel, King of North Wales.   On the
right hand side in the border is a large initial S, which commences the
address with " Sir Watkin Williams Wynn, Bart., M.P.," &c.   This

initial is most elaborate in design, with raised and sunk gold, pearls, &c., and Sir Watkin's crest worked in the centre.   Above and below this initial letter are the arms of another ancestor of the Wynns, Iorwerth Drwyndwn ap Owen Gwynedd, Prince of North Wales, who reigned thirty-two years.   Enclosed by this most elaborate border is the address itself, as far as the words "hunting establishment."   The writing is most elaborate, with raised and sunk gold and emblems of the hunting field, &c., &c.   The third leaf contains the remaining part of the address, enclosed by another border, at the bottom of which is another water-colour view of Sir Watkin's other country residence—Llangedwyn. The remainder of the border is a graceful design of the lily convention-alized, the colouring of which is extremely chaste and beautiful.   The wording on this leaf commences with the words, "The sport you have shown," &c., and terminates with Lord Combermere's signature as chairman.   Then follows the list of names of the members of the Hunt and occupiers of land in Sir Watkin's hunting country, headed by the signature of the Duke of Westminster, with his Grace's crest and coronet at the right hand side; then Lord Hill, Lord Hanmer, Lord Kenyon, &c., &c., placed according to their rank in the peerage, with their crests and coronets to each.   There are over 1,000 names attached to the address, each sheet having a border and sunk mounts.

Sir Watkin, on replying, was received with loud and prolonged cheering.   He said : Ladies and gentlemen, I am glad to see so many ladies here who take an interest in hunting.   I believe we are particu-larly happy in the ladies who do come out in the field.   They do all they can to promote sport, and never to do mischief.   And now, my friends, I beg to thank you all for the kindness of you and many of those I see before me—I might thank their fathers for the kindness they have shown me—for the many pleasant years of happiness in hunting this country.   I may say, that over that long period, I cannot call to mind that I have ever recollected any cause for disagree-ment or unpleasantness having occurred.   We must all own that we hunt on sufferance, and we may therefore thank the occupiers of land, who have assisted us in every way, and have been, I must say, a very kind and long suffering people.   I trust and I hope that I have always done as much as I could to prevent, as much as possible, mischief being done to the fields ; but, of course, gentlemen are jealous of each other, and sometimes a little incautious.   I am exceedingly glad, how-ever, to come back and to see your faces upon this occasion.   You all look better than a lot of old Paschas and Sultans.   I have been looking at stout old fellows riding about on donkeys.   I have now to heartily thank you for the kind reception you have given me. I also thank the oldest friend of my family, Lord Combermere, for the kind manner in which he has made this presentation.

With cheers for Lady Williams Wynn and Lord Combermere, the proceedings ended.

We now come to the last of the " welcomes " and the end of our work. On Friday, May 5, Sir Watkin received the congratulations of his masonic brethren of the Province over which he so worthily occupies the position of Grand Master. The idea was originated by the Shrewsbury Lodges, but the brethren of other lodges were invited to take part in the banquet, which was held at the Lion Hotel, under the presidency of Bro. J. H. Redman, the Worshipful Master of the Salopian Lodge, No. 262. There was a large muster :—amongst others the Deputy Provincial Grand Master, Lord Harlech, was present, and during the proceedings graceful reference was made to the fact that this was the first time he had met his masonic brethren since his elevation to the peerage.

Previously to the banquet, addresses from the two Shrewsbury lodges were presented to the R.W.P.G.M.,—that of the Salopian Lodge, 262, being signed by Bros. Redman, W.M., and his Wardens, E. M. Wakeman and H. Newman ; and the one from the Salopian Lodge of Charity, 117, by the W.M., J. Briscoe Bagnall. To both of these Sir Watkin replied with much feeling.

ERRATA.

In Index for 110 to 128 read 110 to 122.
Page 25. Ten lines from the foot, for *Where* read *There.*
Page 66. Twenty-three lines from the foot, for *Annies* read *Amies.*
Page 67. Second line from the top, for *Wandsworth* read *Wandsford.*

WOODALL AND VENABLES, PRINTERS,

BAILEY-HEAD AND OSWALD-ROAD,

OSWESTRY.

CPSIA information can be obtained at www.ICGtesting.com
Printed in the USA
BVOW012336010513

319672BV00015B/371/P

9 781165 770953